MIXOLOGY FOR BEGINNERS

Sidecar, page 32

MIXOLOGY FOR BEGINNERS

Innovative Craft Cocktails for the Home Bartender

Prairie Rose
Photography by Hélène Dujardin

ROCKRIDGE PRESS

Copyright © 2021 by Rockridge Press, Emeryville, California

No part of this publication may be reproduced, stored in a retrieval system, or transmitted in any form or by any means, electronic, mechanical, photocopying, recording, scanning, or otherwise, except as permitted under Sections 107 or 108 of the 1976 United States Copyright Act, without the prior written permission of the Publisher. Requests to the Publisher for permission should be addressed to the Permissions Department, Rockridge Press, 6005 Shellmound Street, Suite 175, Emeryville, CA 94608.

Limit of Liability/Disclaimer of Warranty: The Publisher and the author make no representations or warranties with respect to the accuracy or completeness of the contents of this work and specifically disclaim all warranties, including without limitation warranties of fitness for a particular purpose. No warranty may be created or extended by sales or promotional materials. The advice and strategies contained herein may not be suitable for every situation. This work is sold with the understanding that the Publisher is not engaged in rendering medical, legal, or other professional advice or services. If professional assistance is required, the services of a competent professional person should be sought. Neither the Publisher nor the author shall be liable for damages arising herefrom. The fact that an individual, organization, or website is referred to in this work as a citation and/or potential source of further information does not mean that the author or the Publisher endorses the information the individual, organization, or website may provide or recommendations they/it may make. Further, readers should be aware that websites listed in this work may have changed or disappeared between when this work was written and when it is read.

For general information on our other products and services or to obtain technical support, please contact our Customer Care Department within the United States at (866) 744-2665, or outside the United States at (510) 253-0500.

Rockridge Press publishes its books in a variety of electronic and print formats. Some content that appears in print may not be available in electronic books, and vice versa.

TRADEMARKS: Rockridge Press and the Rockridge Press logo are trademarks or registered trademarks of Callisto Media Inc. and/or its affiliates, in the United States and other countries, and may not be used without written permission. All other trademarks are the property of their respective owners. Rockridge Press is not associated with any product or vendor mentioned in this book.

Interior and Cover Designer: Erik Jacobsen
Art Producer: Meg Baggott
Editor: Anna Pulley
Production Manager: Holly Haydash

Photography © 2021 Hélène Dujardin. Styling by Anna Hampton.

Author photo courtesy of Eugene Lee.

Paperback ISBN: 978-1-63807-398-7
eBook ISBN: 978-1-63807-631-5
R0

Dedicated to the place that
revealed to me the endless adventures
in cocktails: New York City.

Contents

INTRODUCTION ix

1
Mixology 101
1

2
Brandy
28

3
Champagne & Sparkling Wines
40

4
Gin
52

5
Rum
66

Water Lily, page 59

6
Tequila & Mezcal
78

7
Vodka
90

8
Whisk(e)y
106

9
Wild Cards & Mixed Spirits
120

10
Syrups, Mixers & Modifiers
132

MEASUREMENT CONVERSIONS **144** | RESOURCES **145** | INDEX **147**

Basil Gimlet, page 92

Introduction

When I arrived in New York City mere weeks after turning 22, the first job I landed was behind the bar at a French bistro in Midtown Manhattan. I was hired because I was "a girl." The regulars, a cliquey group of older French men who frequented the restaurant bar nightly, had one request—that the new bartender be of the female persuasion. I was fully qualified in that respect, though I had zero bartending experience! I was stoked to learn the craft of cocktailing. However, most of my drink orders were wine and the occasional pastis and water. If I was lucky, I got an order for a mixed drink. But there was nothing "craft" about those cocktails, and the word "mixology" had yet to enter my lexicon. At that time, in the late 1990s, much of the bar world was still making Margaritas with pre-made sour mix and juice out of a carton.

Little did I know, the cocktail revolution was percolating throughout the city. Dale DeGroff was resurrecting classic cocktails at the Rainbow Room, SoHo's Pravda was turning Dushan Zaric and Jason Kosmas (future founders of Employees Only) into "startenders," and on the Lower East Side, Sasha Petraske was on the verge of opening the seminal speakeasy that came to define the cocktail revival throughout the world, Milk & Honey.

In the aughts, the cocktail scene burst open, and I found myself living in the eye of the boozy storm. While working my day job, I trained at the Wine & Spirit Education Trust (WSET) and took all the cocktail classes in town. I invested in cocktail tomes, curated an impressive home bar, and experimented nightly. In 2013 I started *Bit by a Fox*, a blog devoted to cocktails and drinking culture. When it won *Saveur* magazine's Best Cocktail Blog in 2014, I went from cocktail enthusiast to legit contributor to cocktail culture overnight. In 2018 I launched the *Bit by a Fox Podcast*, where I regularly chat with the movers and shakers in the drinks industry—people from around the world who shape how we drink.

Mixology for Beginners is the result of these last two decades, where fresh ingredients and quality spirits are a given, and the classics are familiar. It is also the result of my experience over that time as an enthusiast, bartender, drinks writer, and cocktail and spirits educator. One of the best parts about working in this industry is introducing the cocktail-curious to their next favorite concoction to make at home and helping to spark the creative mixologist within. So, I'm especially stoked to be writing this book for those people in particular.

The cocktails in this book are approachable and fun. You'll find timeless classics and improved-upon favorites as well as fresh innovations. Whether you're a beginner or an experienced cocktailian, this book will give you the tools to up your game, create your own inventive concoctions, and become the expert home bartender you've always dreamed of being.

CHAPTER 1
Mixology 101

Welcome fellow cocktail enthusiasts, hard-core nerds, budding home mixologists, and everything in between! In this first chapter, we'll explore what characterizes a *craft cocktail*. You'll get recommendations for essential bar tools and glassware, and advice for building your home bar. We'll cover common cocktail terms and go over the simple techniques that help demystify craft cocktail creation so you can hone your skills and learn some things along the way.

What Is a Craft Cocktail?

America's craft cocktail revival came into its own in the early aughts. It coincided with the farm-to-table movement and the craft distilling boom and had us embracing fresh ingredients and high-quality spirits. Craft cocktails are the culmination of this classic cocktail renaissance, with an attention to detail, influenced by the past as well as current trends.

In the early days of the cocktail revival, we rediscovered classic cocktails and uncovered long-forgotten cocktail history. We often eschewed sour mix concoctions with sub-par ingredients in favor of pre-prohibition-style drinks crafted by a mustachioed bartender straight out of the 1800s. Bartenders (and food and drink writers) resurrected the 19th-century term *mixologist*, elevating the job of mixing drinks back to its original art form, where skill and craftsmanship took center stage.

This resurgence of classic drinks, secret speakeasies, and twirly mustaches has since gone through an evolution. The craft movement, now well into its second decade, elevated the cocktail, created artisans out of bartenders, and revealed a history that pointed us toward the future. We are now on the other side of that cocktail nostalgia, but have held onto a basic understanding of that classic palate. Now is the new, golden age of cocktails, in which we draw inspiration from the classics, but continue to innovate.

We still care about quality ingredients, creative flavor profiles, and attention to detail. We've just relaxed a bit. We don't need to take ourselves too seriously to execute an excellent drink. We can embrace the playful cocktails of the '70s, '80s, and '90s that are not often associated with the craft movement and make them with fresh ingredients *and* a fresh new take.

The cocktails in this book are a mix of those fun and familiar interpretations raised to the level of craft as well as updated classics and original creations. There will also be tips on how you can put your creative twist on your favorites and how to easily conceptualize flavor combinations.

The Lingo

A working knowledge of bartending lingo is essential for the home mixologist. The following terms will help get you started.

ABV/proof: Alcohol by volume (ABV) is the standard measurement of the alcohol content of a distilled spirit used worldwide. In the United States, you can calculate the proof by doubling the ABV. For example, a spirit that contains 40 percent ABV is 80 proof.

Aperitif: Often a less alcoholic drink, traditionally served before dinner to stimulate the appetite. Fortified wines, vermouths, dry sparkling wines, and cocktails containing these ingredients, are commonly thought of as aperitifs.

Bitters: An herbal tincture made up of a concentration of bitter botanicals, spices, and roots. Cocktail bitters are used in small doses to add depth of flavor and complexity to a drink.

Build: To assemble a drink's ingredients directly in the glass without having to shake. This can be done with or without ice.

Dash: The smallest amount dispensed from a dasher or bitters bottle, often used to measure the amount of bitters added to a cocktail recipe.

Express: To extract the aromatic oils of a citrus peel by squeezing the fruit rind over the cocktail for added flavor.

Float: The technique of delicately adding about a tablespoon, or half an ounce, of spirit or another ingredient as a layer on top of a drink.

Garnish: An often-edible addition to a drink. A garnish can also be a vital ingredient, such as cocktail cherries in a Manhattan, olives or a twist in a martini, or celery in a Bloody Mary. Flowers, herbs, or a sugared or salted rim are also considered garnishes that enhance the drink experience.

Liqueur: A sweetened, distilled spirit, historically descended from medicinal spirits and traditionally infused with herbs and botanicals. These are often used as modifiers in a cocktail.

Mixer: Non-alcoholic beverage, such as juice or soda, that complements and enhances a spirit in a cocktail.

Modifier: A liqueur or a fortified wine that complements and balances the base spirit in a cocktail. The addition of a modifier can often add depth of flavor and sweetness.

Muddle: To mash ingredients such as herbs and fruit to release their oils and flavors.

Neat: A one-spirit drink, served at room temperature, without ice.

Rocks/on the rocks: A drink served with ice.

Shaken: A cocktail that contains juice, dairy, or eggs needs to be shaken to integrate all of the ingredients. Shaking helps break down the ice, incorporate air, and cool and dilute the drink.

Stirred: A cocktail comprised of mostly spirits and no juice is stirred over ice to cool and dilute the drink.

Strain: After shaking or stirring a cocktail, the process of using a cocktail strainer to separate the liquid from the ice and other ingredients when pouring into a glass.

Top with: To add a splash of a carbonated beverage, such as sparkling wine, club soda, or ginger ale, at the very end of a cocktail build.

Up/straight-up: A shaken or stirred drink, served chilled, without ice.

Building Your Bar

Here is where you'll learn about the key ingredients and tools you need to have to craft your own cocktails.

The Liquids

As a cocktail and spirits expert, I constantly get asked to list the most important bottles to have on hand. The key ingredients I recommend directly apply to the cocktails featured in this book. They are also invaluable items to have in your home bar to make craft cocktails at any time. You can cultivate a well-stocked bar without spending a fortune or sacrificing shelf space. These products should be of good quality, economical, and versatile.

LIQUORS

Whisk(e)y (bourbon, rye, scotch): Whiskey is a distilled spirit made from a fermented mash of grain such as rye, barley, or corn. Styles of whiskey, such as bourbon, rye, or scotch, vary because of the different production methods and grains used.

> **Bottles:** *For bourbon, try Four Roses, Buffalo Trace, Maker's Mark, or George Dickel Bottled in Bond; for rye, try Old Overholt, Rittenhouse Rye, Jack Daniel's Rye, or Catoctin Creek.*

Brandy: Brandy is a fruit distillate made by fermenting wine, distilling it into a higher-alcohol spirit, and usually aging it in oak casks. Grape-based brandies such as cognac and Armagnac account for more than 90 percent of the world's production.

> **Bottles:** *For cognac, try H by Hine, Pierre Ferrand 1840, or Martell VS; for American-made brandy, try Copper & Kings, Bertoux Brandy, or Argonaut.*

Vodka: Vodka is a clear, unaged, neutral spirit made from any ingredient that contains fermentable sugars, most often grain, potatoes, or fruit.

> **Bottles:** *Look for Aylesbury Duck, Grey Goose, Hangar 1 Vodka, and Ketel One.*

Gin: Gin is a neutral spirit flavored with juniper berries and other aromatic botanicals.

> **Bottles:** *Try a classic London dry-style gin, such as Plymouth or Sipsmith, or American brands Aviation or Fords Gin.*

Rum: Rum is a distilled spirit made from a sugar product such as cane juice, molasses, or sugarcane by-products.

> **Bottles:** *Look for The Real McCoy 3-Year-Aged Silver Rum, Plantation Grande Reserve 5 Years, or Mount Gay Black Barrel Rum. For an aged rum, try Diplomático Reserva Exclusiva from Venezuela.*

Tequila and Mezcal: Tequila can only be made from blue Weber agave in designated regions in Mexico. Mezcal is any agave-based distilled spirit, which includes tequila.

> **Bottles:** *For tequila, try Cazadores Blanco or Espolòn; for mezcal, try Montelobos or Del Maguey Vida.*

LIQUEURS, FORTIFIED WINES, AND SPARKLING WINES

Fruit Liqueurs: Fruit liqueurs are sweetened, distilled spirits that use fruit as their main flavoring component. Orange liqueurs are some of the most popular. Curaçao and triple sec are fairly interchangeable orange liqueurs.

Bottles: Cointreau, Grand Marnier, maraschino, crème de cassis, blackberry liqueur, Midori, and Limoncello (page 140).

Amaro and Bitter Aperitivo Liqueurs: *Amaro* is Italian for "bitter." From the dark, rich, and medicinal Fernet-Branca to the sweet, candied-orange flavor profile of Aperol, these herbaceous digestifs range greatly in style. In Italy, amari have long been reserved as stand-alone before- or after-dinner sippers. However, in the current craft cocktail age, they are favorite flavor enhancers, or modifiers, in cocktails.

Bottles: Campari, Aperol, Lo-Fi Gentian Amaro, Meletti, Averna.

Herbal and Botanical Liqueurs: Most liqueurs have some kind of herbal or botanical infusion. These liqueurs use specific botanicals and herbs to give them a definitive flavor profile, from anise and wormwood, to mint, coffee, and elderflowers.

Bottles: Bénédictine, Chartreuse, Galliano, absinthe, crème de violette, elderflower liqueur, ginger liqueur, crème de cacao, crème de menthe, Coffee Liqueur (page 142).

Fortified Wines: A fortified wine is a wine base with a distilled spirit such as brandy added to it. Common types are port, sherry, and madeira. Vermouth is a fortified wine aromatized with herbs, spices, and sometimes fruit.

   Bottles: *Dolin, Carpano Antica Formula, Noilly Prat, Lillet, Suze.*

Champagne/Sparkling Wines: A sparkling wine gets its bubbles from carbon dioxide from either a natural fermentation in the bottle, as with the Champagne method, outside the bottle in a large tank, or by injection.

   Bottles: *Piper-Heidsieck Brut Champagne, Gruet Brut, La Marca, Mionetto, Freixenet Cordon Negro.*

Mixers and Infusions

A cocktail is only as good as the sum of its parts. If you use quality spirits, it only makes sense to use fresh juice and well-made mixers and sweeteners. These ingredients are also essential in any well-stocked bar.

SWEETENERS

Agave nectar: Complements agave-based spirits like tequila and mezcal.

Chocolate syrup: Often used for dessert-style cocktails

Coffee Syrup (page 138): A versatile syrup that can pair with tequila as well as whiskey

Earl Grey Syrup (page 137): A simple tea infusion with a unique bergamot flavor

Fruit marmalades and preserves: Jams and marmalades can take the place of simple syrup.

Ginger Syrup (page 136): An easy-to-make syrup that adds sweetness and spice

Grenadine: A common cocktail ingredient known for its bright red color and pomegranate base

Maple syrup: Pairs exceptionally well in whiskey cocktails

Orgeat Syrup (page 139): Often used in classic and tiki-style cocktails

Simple Syrup (page 135): The most basic and widely used of all cocktail sweeteners

SODAS

Bubbly water:
- **Club soda:** Has added minerals and sodium; most commonly used in cocktails
- **Seltzer or sparkling water:** Simple, carbonated water
- **Sparkling mineral water:** Naturally carbonated and sourced from a spring, containing dissolved minerals such as potassium, magnesium, and calcium

Ginger ale/ginger beer: Using a ginger beer or ale with a base spirit makes a mule or buck cocktail

Grapefruit soda: Commonly used to make Palomas

Tonic water: Choose good-quality tonic water like Fever-Tree or Q Tonic.

FRUIT AND JUICES

Make sure to use freshly squeezed juice when possible.

Apple cider: Fall and winter cocktails often call for an apple cider mixer.

Coconut water: Adds a nice mouthfeel and can soften a drink's overall flavor profile

Cranberry juice: Can add vibrant red color and tartness to a drink

Grapefruit juice: Ranges in sweetness and acidity; this can take the place of lemon or lime in a cocktail

Lemon juice: Arguably the most important and versatile fresh juice to have on hand

Lime juice: Slightly more bitter and less sweet than lemon

Mango purée: For a sweet, tropical infusion in a cocktail

Orange juice: Freshly squeezed, this can add a bright citrus quality and sweetness.

Passion fruit purée: Perfumy, sweet, and slightly tart

Pineapple juice: Used in tropical drinks to add sweetness and acidity

ADDITIONAL MIXER INGREDIENTS

Apple cider vinegar: Can take the place of citrus as the acidic part of a cocktail

Bloody Mary Mix (page 141): A combination of tomato juice, spices, and seasoning

Egg white: An optional ingredient in many sour-type cocktails; adds a frothy top and silky mouthfeel

Espresso: Freshly made is best when using this in cocktails

Heavy (whipping) cream: Used in small quantities, this can help diffuse intense flavors and add a rich quality to a cocktail.

Vanilla ice cream: Turn a cream-based cocktail into a dessert with this addition.

Garnishes

An edible olive or cherry, a well-sculpted citrus rind, a sugared rim, and even cocktail bitters are all considered cocktail garnishes. These can add to the aesthetics of the drink as well as the flavor and overall experience.

Bitters: These are also known as "the bartender's spice rack."

- **Aromatic bitters:** Angostura and Peychaud's are traditional aromatic bitters brands
- **Chocolate bitters**
- **Orange bitters**

Candied ginger: A by-product of making Ginger Syrup (page 136) is leftover ginger. This can easily be turned into homemade candied ginger.

Cocktail cherries: These include maraschino, brandied, and whiskey. Stay away from the fake, neon-red cherries, and instead go for brands like the classic Luxardo Maraschino, elegant Amarena Fabbri Wild Cherries, and boozy Dirty Sue Whiskey Cherries.

Coffee beans: Cocktails that contain espresso, Coffee Syrup (page 138), or Coffee Liqueur (page 142) are often garnished with coffee beans for aromatic and aesthetic purposes.

Fresh fruit: Seasonal fruit garnishes can be decorative, edible, and an essential ingredient in cocktail recipes.

Fresh herbs: The summer and spring seasons often call for fresh herb garnishes in a cocktail, such as mint, basil, rosemary, thyme, or lavender—crucial ingredients in the overall drink.

Granulated sugar: Some cocktail recipes call for loose sugar to muddle with bitters, herbs, and fruit.

Olives/pickles/pickled veggies: Savory cocktails such as the Bloody Mary (page 95) require such garnishes.

Spices: Spices such as nutmeg, cinnamon, and cayenne can be used as a finishing garnish when building a cocktail or on the rim of the glass with a combination of sugar or salt.

ICE, ICE BABY

One of the most essential ingredients in a cocktail is also the least expensive: ice! Just as quality spirits and fresh ingredients are important when making well-crafted cocktails, good ice is critical. Ice cools the drink down when shaking or stirring, and the dilution it imparts during this process becomes a fundamental part of the drink. Who doesn't love a big sexy rock in their old fashioned? Not only is it aesthetically pleasing, but a larger cube will also melt more slowly, dilute the drink more gradually, and maintain an ideal sipping temperature for longer. Use clean, filtered, or even purified water to make neutral-tasting ice that won't impart any flavors as it melts. Silicone cube trays come in all sizes and shapes in order to fit that rocks or highball glass flawlessly.

Sugar cubes: Raw or brown cubes work well for cocktails.

Vegetables: Some cocktails call for veggies like cucumber, jalapeño, celery, or tomato.

The Glasses

The cocktail glass is incredibly important to the overall experience. After all, we taste with our eyes before we even have a chance to get liquid to our lips. However, do you really need a different glass for every variation of cocktail? While it's fun to have a proper copper mug for a Moscow Mule or a traditional Mint Julep cup when the Kentucky Derby rolls around, having the "correct" vessel on hand can be costly and take up unnecessary shelf space. As a vintage glassware junkie, I know how out of hand it can get! I've pared this list down to the most essential and interchangeable glassware you'll need for an enviable home bar.

Coupe glass: An elegant, stemmed glass used for drinks served without ice. The classic champagne coupe is a craft cocktail favorite and has taken the place of the V-shaped martini glass in most craft cocktail bars.

Highball/Collins glass: A tall, slim glass used to serve drinks with ice. It is large enough to accommodate a good amount of mixer, often soda.

Nick and Nora glass: Named after Nick and Nora Charles, the fictional husband-and-wife team from a series of 1930s detective movies. They sipped copious martinis out of this glass. Like the coupe, these are also stemmed and used for straight-up drinks, but are often smaller, narrower, and more bell-shaped.

Rocks/old fashioned glass: Used for single spirits served on their own, either neat or on the rocks. These are often used for more spirit-forward, stirred cocktails served over ice, such as an old fashioned, as its name implies.

Wine glass: With stems or stemless, these are great for punch, wine-based cocktails, and aperitif cocktails such as an Italiano Spritz (page 42) or Negroni Sbagliato (page 47).

The Tools

Having the right bar tools makes crafting cocktails at home a lot easier, *and you'll* feel like a pro. You don't need to spend a fortune to trick out your home bar. I've included the essentials that will help when making the recipes in this book and beyond.

Bar spoon: This elegant, long-handled spoon is used to stir cocktails in a tall mixing glass, spoon out cocktail cherries or olives, and measure a teaspoon of ingredients.

Citrus squeezer: One of the most important bar tools is a hand-held citrus squeezer that extracts juice easily and efficiently.

 **Cocktail shaker:** Shaking a cocktail is necessary if the recipe includes any juice, dairy, or eggs. The cobbler shaker is an all-in-one shaker that includes a built-in strainer and is most commonly used in home bars. The two-piece Boston shaker is used by most professional bartenders and it has one large tin that fits over a smaller mixing glass or tin.

 Jigger: This tool will measure ingredients precisely—the single most important step when crafting cocktails.

 Mixing glass: Cocktails that are spirit-forward, such as Martinis or Manhattans, will need to be stirred over ice. A proper mixing glass is sturdy and can hold ice and multiple cocktails.

 Muddler: When building a cocktail, this tool is used to mash herbs and fruit to release their flavors and oils.

 Paring knife: Useful for cutting fresh fruit, veggies, or herbs.

 Peeler: Use this to precisely peel the skin from citrus fruits.

Strainer: A Hawthorne strainer fits snugly over a mixing glass or a Boston shaker tin and catches the ice and large ingredients you want separated. A fine-mesh strainer is used for double straining muddled cocktails and drinks that include fine ingredients such as seeds and herbs.

TOOL HACKS

You can, of course, shake up craft cocktail-worthy drinks even if you don't have a fully equipped home bar. Here are four work-arounds that will make the most out of what you may already have in your kitchen.

No shaker? A wide-mouthed water bottle, protein shaker cup, or a medium mason jar with a sealable lid can work as a makeshift shaker in a pinch. Preparing a picnic or outdoor adventure? These can also be used as to-go cocktail containers!

No muddler? Use the handle of a wooden spoon or spatula.

No jigger? Most people reach for a shot glass in place of a jigger to measure their cocktail ingredients, but not all shot glasses are created equal. Some measure 1½ ounces, while others are 2 ounces. To be safe, use the always-reliable tablespoon, which measures ½ ounce.

No strainer? If you're a tea or coffee drinker, you may already have a strainer for your cocktail. Open tea strainers work in place of a fine-mesh strainer to catch the small bits you don't want in the glass. A coffee filter in a cone can work in the same way.

The Methods

The techniques you choose when putting a cocktail together, whether you are shaking, stirring, or building a cocktail in the glass, will greatly influence the final outcome, altering the taste, texture, and dilution level. Here are some guidelines for each method.

Building in the glass: Highball-style mixed drinks with a base spirit and mixer, such as Gin and Tonics or Moscow Mules, are usually prepped and served in the glass.

Double straining: Straining a shaken or stirred cocktail helps separate the liquid from the ice and other ingredients. When there are still smaller bits of unwanted ingredients, a double strain using a fine-mesh strainer is required.

Dry shaking: Shaking a cocktail without ice. When a cocktail contains egg white or a full egg, you can add a "dry" shake before adding ice to your shaker for a second "wet" shake. The result will be a silky mouthfeel and white lather topping.

Rinsing/washing the glass: This process involves pouring a spirit into a glass, swirling the liquid around to coat the entire inside to the rim, and then discarding the liquid. An absinthe rinse is often called for when making a Sazerac.

Rolling: Pouring the cocktail from one shaker tin to another. This method is applied when stirring is not enough and shaking is too much. The Bloody Mary often calls for this method to get the right amount of dilution and aeration without agitating the drink too much.

Shaking: A cocktail is shaken when it contains juice, dairy, or eggs. Shaking blends the ingredients and incorporates air for a frothy texture. The ice also imparts dilution and cools down the drink. Sour cocktails such as Sidecars, Margaritas, and Daiquiris all need to be shaken.

Stirring: Spirit-forward cocktails that don't contain juice, such as Manhattans and Negronis, are stirred over ice. This is to gently integrate the ingredients while imparting dilution and cooling down the drink.

The Flourishes

Everything that goes into a cocktail recipe is important, including the distinctive flair that can make it especially unique. These finishing touches to a cocktail will impress your guests and give it that extra wow factor.

Citrus twist or spiral: Use ripe fruit with tough, clean skin. When peeling the skin, avoid as much white pith as possible. Shape into a twist or a tight spiral. To express the oils, twist over the glass, skin-side down.

Flame a peel: Use room-temperature citrus with dimpled, oily skin. Peel a large swath of skin, then light a match, holding the peel skin-side down over the finished drink, near the flame. Pinch from the center of the peel to express the oils onto the flame.

Rim a glass with citrus: Rub the peel side of the citrus against the outside rim of a glass.

Create a sugar or salt rim: Cover a small, flat dish with sugar, salt, or a spice mixture. Use a citrus wedge to wet the rim of a glass. Dip the glass rim-side down into the dish and coat with the sugar, salt, or spice mixture.

Spank herbs: To wake up herbs like mint and basil, lightly slap them on the outside of your hand before adding as a garnish.

Building a Cocktail

Every aspect of building a cocktail is important, from prepping glassware and tools to deciding whether to shake or stir. This is a step-by-step guide for building a cocktail from start to finish.

Step 1: Prep. Make sure you have all of the tools and ingredients you'll need for the cocktail, including the ice, glassware, and garnishes.

Step 2: Chill the glass. To prepare for a properly chilled cocktail, chill the glass you'll be using by filling it with ice and water or putting it in the freezer.

Step 3: Ready the mixer or shaker. If the recipe calls for all spirits, use a mixing glass to stir over ice. If there is juice in the recipe, use a shaker tin to help integrate the ingredients.

Step 4: Add ingredients. Measure the ingredients into the mixing glass or shaker tin, following the order in the recipe.

Step 5: Add ice. In the mixing glass or shaker tin, add fresh, clear ice cubes.

Step 6: Shake or stir. Stir the mixing glass with ice until well chilled and diluted, about 20 rotations. Or seal the shaker and shake until the outside of the tin is cold to the touch and frosty.

Step 7: Strain. Dump the ice from the chilled glass and add fresh ice if the recipe calls for "on the rocks." Strain from the mixing glass or shaker tin into the cocktail glass.

Step 8: Top with bubbles. If adding carbonated ingredients (soda, sparkling wine, or tonic), top the drink with the stated amount and stir to integrate.

Step 9: Garnish. Add the final touch to the cocktail with a fresh garnish or twist.

Inventing Your Own Signature Cocktail

So, you'd like to invent your very own cocktail from scratch. But where do you start? While there is no doubt that cocktail creation is a skill, and there's a reason we leave overly complicated tipples to the professionals, coming up with a delicious cocktail recipe might just be easier than you think.

Always remember that balance is key to any well-made drink. And when it comes to the endless family of "sour cocktails"—Margarita, Daiquiri, Whiskey Sour, Sidecar, Gimlet—the right ratio of sweet, sour, and strong is just as important as the quality of the ingredients. These iconic three-ingredient cocktails are the best examples of how you can swap out one or two ingredients using a formula and come up with an entirely different drink.

The basic ratio for most any cocktail that includes citrus is 2:1:1—That's two parts strong (base spirit), one part sweet (can include a sweet liqueur or syrup), and one part sour (most often fresh lemon or lime juice). The simplest conversion for jigger measurements is 2 ounces, 1 ounce, and 1 ounce. But you can halve that or tweak it to 1½ ounces, ¾ ounce, ¾ ounce (the same ratio), depending on how boozy you're feeling!

This "golden ratio" formula is ideal for when you might not have all the necessary ingredients to make a specific cocktail but would like to improvise with what you *do* have. If you'd like to make a Margarita, for instance, and have tequila and lime but no triple sec or orange liqueur, you can substitute a simple syrup, orgeat (for a rich, nutty flavor), or better yet, agave syrup in its place. You can even swap in another liqueur for the triple sec. I'm a huge fan of using ginger liqueur in my Margaritas for some extra spice. What's most likely the case is that you have a leftover bottle of triple sec but no tequila. But if there's gin or vodka in the house, you're in luck; You can now make a Gin Gimlet or a Kamikaze instead. The variations are endless!

As with all cocktail experimentations, taste is subjective, and you may have to fiddle with the ratios, depending on the ingredients you use. But using this golden ratio formula is an excellent jumping-off point. You can now feel confident exploring flavor combinations within a structure you know is fairly fail-safe. Happy experimenting!

HOW TO NAME A DRINK

Recipe testing and developing an original cocktail is only half the fun. The other creative step that makes your cocktail legit is naming it! There are several approaches to bestowing an original moniker on your new precious concoction. I've broken it down into five categories.

The Star Ingredient: Whiskey Sour, Aperol Spritz, Mint Julep

When the featured ingredient is the best descriptor, add the star ingredient to the name.

The Medicine: Penicillin, Painkiller, Mind Eraser

When your cocktail is the medicine and the cure, write a script for that!

The Personality: Negroni (Count Negroni), Bellini (Italian painter Giovanni Bellini), Kir Royale (French Resistance fighter and politician Félix Kir)

When a historic celebrity inspires your new creation, be sure to brand it.

The Aesthetics: Tequila Sunrise, Bloody Mary, Aviation (crème de violette gives the cocktail a pale, sky blue color)

When the overall look of your drink informs the cocktail name, your creativity can shine.

The Political Event: Cuba Libre ("Free Cuba" was the slogan of the Cuban independence movement during the Spanish-American War); Ward 8 (the district in Boston that helped politician Martin M. Lomasney win his race)

When you want to honor a historic moment in time, you can give it a nod with a memorable name.

Bloody Mary, page 95

About the Recipes

Now that you've gone over the lingo, the home bar must-haves, and the techniques, tips, and hacks to creating craft cocktails at home, it's time to start putting all of that info to work to create some deliciousness of your own!

All the recipes in this book are categorized by the base spirit, so you can jump to your favorite liquor, or what you may have on hand at the moment, for initial inspiration. There are profile labels (Strong, Sweet, Dry, and Sour) listed below each cocktail's name for easy reference.

The collection of cocktail recipes I've gathered for this book are a mix of classics everyone should know, creations from acclaimed bartenders and well-established bars from around the world as well as original recipes of my own. Some of the classic cocktails I've included have been updated with a simple twist or a slight refinement—subtle enough that you'll still recognize your favorites. There will always be options and suggestions to swap out a spirit, mixer, or garnish to create your own variation on these drinks and eventually make them your own. Note that each recipe is designed to yield one drink unless otherwise noted. Let's get shaking!

Mezcal Paloma, page 85

CHAPTER 2

Brandy

Brandy was an essential ingredient in pre-Prohibition recipes, and pivotal at the onset of cocktail culture. Many classic cocktails that today we think of as whiskey-based were originally made with brandy, such as the Mint Julep and Sazerac. Brandy is an incredibly versatile spirit. It can be treated as any other brown spirit in stiff, stirred drinks, such as a Vieux Carré (page 117), and it lends itself well to sour cocktails like the Sidecar (page 32) because of its bright fruit aromas and high acidity.

Jack Rosé Spritz 31

Sidecar 32

Brandy Highball 33

Coffee Sazerac 34

Vanderbilt Stinger 36

Corpse Reviver No. 1 38

Brandy Alexander 39

Jack Rosé Spritz

Sweet, Sour

The Jack Rose dates to the early 1900s and was especially popular in the '20s and '30s. It's most likely named after the applejack brandy used as the base spirit, and the rose-colored hue from the grenadine. This contemporary take adds a topper of sparkling rosé wine and is served on the rocks, giving it a lighter, aperitif feel. For a traditional Jack Rose, simply omit the rosé and double up on the rest of the ingredients.

1 ounce applejack brandy

½ ounce freshly squeezed lemon juice

½ ounce grenadine

2 or 3 ounces sparkling rosé wine

Lemon twist, for garnish

Measure the brandy, lemon juice, and grenadine into an ice-filled shaker. Shake until well chilled. Strain into an ice-filled wine glass. Top with sparkling rosé wine. Garnish with a lemon twist.

DID YOU KNOW? In Ernest Hemingway's 1926 novel *The Sun Also Rises*, the main character, Jake Barnes, sips on a Jack Rose cocktail while waiting in a hotel bar in Paris.

Tools needed: Stemmed wine glass, jigger, citrus squeezer, shaker, strainer, peeler

Sidecar

Sweet, Sour

The Sidecar is part of the "sour" family of drinks, which includes the Margarita, Whiskey Sour, and Daiquiri. This style of cocktail has roots in the punch British sailors drank in the 1600s. In 1862, the Brandy Crusta was featured in the first cocktail book from "Professor" Jerry Thomas, who refined this punch-style drink to include orange curaçao.

Lemon wedge, for rim

1 teaspoon sugar, for rim

2 ounces brandy

1 ounce freshly squeezed lemon juice

1 ounce orange liqueur

Lemon twist, for garnish

To rim the glass, cut a slice into the lemon wedge and swipe it around half of the glass. Measure the sugar onto a small plate, dip half the glass into the mixture, and set aside. Measure the brandy, lemon juice, and orange liqueur into an ice-filled shaker. Shake until well chilled. Strain into the prepared glass. Express lemon oils from the twist over the glass and add it to the glass.

VARIATION TIP: For a bright kick of ginger, substitute the orange liqueur for Ginger Syrup (page 136).

> **Tools needed:** Coupe glass, paring knife, bar spoon, small plate, jigger, citrus squeezer, shaker, strainer, peeler

Brandy Highball

Strong, Dry

The highball is at once classic and modern. The original "tall" drink that came into favor in the late 1800s consisted simply of spirit, ice, and a carbonated mixer. Some popular examples of highballs are the Gin and Tonic, Whiskey and Ginger, and Rum and Coke. The Brandy and Soda combination was a favorite in England in the early 19th century, and in recent years has made a fashionable return around the world.

2 ounces brandy

2 to 4 dashes orange bitters

4 ounces club soda

Lemon twist, for garnish

Measure the brandy directly into an ice-filled highball glass. Add bitters and top with soda. Stir until chilled. Garnish with a lemon twist.

VARIATION TIP: The highball recipe is one of the most versatile in terms of swapping out a spirit, mixer, and garnish. If this version is too dry for you, try it with a quality tonic or ginger ale (for a Horse's Neck cocktail). You can even substitute the orange bitters with rhubarb or cherry versions for a subtle change.

> **Tools needed:** Highball/Collins glass, jigger, bar spoon, peeler

Coffee Sazerac

Strong

The creation of the Sazerac, one of the oldest known American cocktails, is the subject of much debate. What we do know is that it originated in New Orleans around the mid-1800s, and apothecary owner Antoine Amédée Peychaud had a hand in its formation. The name came from the main ingredient, a popular brand of cognac called Sazerac de Forge et Fils. This twist on the original recipe swaps out the traditional sugar cube for Coffee Syrup (page 138). The sweet smokiness and cocoa in the syrup complements the dried fruit and spices in the brandy, while tempering the licorice notes from the absinthe rinse. The orange twist in place of the traditional lemon plays up the warm flavors.

1 teaspoon absinthe

2½ ounces brandy

¼ ounce Coffee Syrup (page 138)

4 dashes bitters

Orange twist, for garnish

Tools needed: Rocks/old fashioned glass, bar spoon, jigger, mixing glass, strainer, peeler

Pour the absinthe into the rocks glass, swirl it around to coat the inside, and dump out any remaining liquid, then set aside. Measure the brandy, coffee syrup, and bitters into a mixing glass with ice. Stir until chilled. Place a large ice cube in a rocks glass and strain the liquid from the shaker into the glass. Express orange oils from the twist into the drink and discard, or add the twist to the glass.

VARIATION TIP: Most Sazeracs you'll find on menus today are made with whiskey, and this can easily be swapped out. A rye whiskey and a robust brandy split (1¼ ounces each) make for a delightful combination. In case you don't have coffee syrup on hand, you can substitute maple syrup. This variation can benefit from a flamed orange peel (see page 21). For a more traditional Sazerac, muddle a sugar cube in the mixing glass with the brandy and bitters, stir and strain, and garnish with a lemon twist.

Vanderbilt Stinger

Strong, Sweet

The stinger, traditionally a two-ingredient cocktail made with just brandy and white crème de menthe, has always invoked a sense of sophistication. It was a favorite of high society from the time of its inception in the late 1800s through the height of its popularity in the '20s, and even up until the 1970s. It fell out of favor for a number of decades, but has since been dusted off by some notable bartenders and revived, thanks to the recent cocktail resurgence. This version takes inspiration from the past. Legend has it that in the early 1920s, New York millionaire Reginald "Reggie" Vanderbilt (Gloria's dad), served Stingers at his nightly cocktail hours and included a dash of absinthe.

2 ounces brandy

¾ ounce white crème de menthe

½ teaspoon absinthe

Fresh mint sprig, for garnish

Measure the brandy, white crème de menthe, and absinthe into an ice-filled shaker. Shake until well chilled. Strain into a chilled Nick and Nora glass. Garnish with a sprig of mint.

PREP TIP: While this cocktail is made up only of spirits, the Stinger is typically a shaken cocktail, perhaps because of the flourish in the preparation, or the fact that this drink works best when it is icy cold. Whatever the reason, we're sticking with this classic construction!

> **Tools needed:** Nick and Nora glass, jigger, bar spoon, shaker, strainer

Corpse Reviver No.1

Strong

The cheekily named Corpse Reviver cocktails were originally created as a sort of "hair of the dog" remedy after a long night of imbibing. This recipe first appeared in the 1930 edition of *The Savoy Cocktail Book* by Harry Craddock—a collection of the most popular cocktails of the time at the Savoy Hotel in London. Craddock wrote of the Corpse Reviver No. 1: "To be taken before 11 a.m., or whenever steam and energy are needed." This may be a bit boozy for breakfast nowadays, as it is closer to a sort of Brandy Manhattan. I would recommend this as a before- or after-dinner sipper.

1 ounce cognac

1 ounce Calvados or apple brandy

½ ounce sweet vermouth

Orange twist, for garnish

Measure the cognac, apple brandy, and sweet vermouth into a mixing glass and fill with ice. Stir until well chilled. Strain into a chilled coupe glass. Express orange oils from the twist into the drink and add the twist to the glass.

Tools needed: Coupe glass, jigger, mixing glass, bar spoon, strainer, peeler

Brandy Alexander

Sweet, Strong

The Brandy Alexander is a classic three-ingredient cocktail that is literally dessert in a cocktail glass. The original iteration of this drink, created just after the turn of the twentieth century, was equal parts gin, crème de cacao, and cream, and referred to simply as the Alexander. Brandy took the place of the gin about 20 years later, and the Brandy Alexander was born. The recipe is often shown as equal parts, but I prefer just a touch more brandy to balance out the richness of the other ingredients. Because of the cream, this is a shaken cocktail.

1½ ounces brandy

1 ounce dark crème de cacao

1 ounce heavy (whipping) cream

Freshly grated nutmeg, for garnish

Tools needed: Coupe glass, jigger, shaker, strainer

Measure the brandy, dark crème de cacao, and heavy cream into an ice-filled shaker. Shake until well chilled. Strain into a chilled coupe glass. Garnish with nutmeg.

DID YOU KNOW? The Brandy Alexander was reportedly John Lennon's favorite cocktail, introduced to him by the singer-songwriter Harry Nilsson. When they were both famously tossed from the iconic Los Angeles music venue Troubadour for heckling the Smothers Brothers in the 1970s, Lennon blamed it on the consumption of too many of these rich, brandy cocktails.

CHAPTER 3

Champagne & Sparkling Wines

Want to add some sparkle to your cocktails? Champagne and sparkling wine cocktails are some of the most festive, fun, and easy sippers around. One of the best ways to liven up and *lighten* up a drink is to add bubbles! While sparkling wine conjures a sense of celebration, these cocktails can be everyday pre-dinner drinks, enjoyed on their own or as an elegant complement to a meal. Dry sparkling wine not only adds effervescence to a cocktail, but it can also reduce sweetness, add depth of flavor, and soften and integrate the other ingredients.

Italiano Spritz 42

French 75 43

Mango con Chili Bellini 45

Blood Orange Mimosa 46

Negroni Sbagliato (Mistaken Negroni) 47

Old Cuban 48

Seelbach 49

Twinkle 50

Italiano Spritz

Sweet

Aperitivo hour in Italy is a rich pre-dinner tradition meant to wind down the day and whet the appetite. Its star beverage, the spritz, has become a global obsession in recent years. And there's a reason: They're light, refreshing, low in alcohol, and tasty! The orangey, bittersweet quality of the Italian-style aperitivo liqueur is mellowed by the chilled Prosecco and touch of soda, making for an easy-drinking aperitif, or anytime drink.

2 ounces bitter aperitivo liqueur (such as Aperol or Campari)

3 or 4 ounces Prosecco or sparkling wine

1 ounce club soda

Orange slice or wheel, for garnish

Fill a wine glass with ice. Measure and add the liqueur, Prosecco, and soda and stir. Garnish with the orange slice.

VARIATION TIP: Though this cocktail is most commonly referred to as the Aperol Spritz, in Italy they tend to use a variety of Italian aperitivo liqueurs. There are some international brands that all have slightly different qualities—some less bitter or less sweet, or more herbaceous—that can work well in a spritz.

Tools needed: Stemmed wine glass, jigger, bar spoon, paring knife

French 75

Dry

The French 75 has a reputation. It has long been considered one of the most delicious sparkling wine cocktails ever created, and yet it is also known to pack quite the punch. Named after a light field gun used frequently by the French army during World War I, in reference to its powerful... effects, this sparkler dates back to the early 1900s. Early versions cite cognac instead of gin as the base spirit. You can change this up depending on the seasons.

1 ounce gin

½ ounce freshly squeezed lemon juice

½ ounce Simple Syrup (page 135)

3 ounces sparkling wine

Lemon twist, for garnish

Tools needed: Coupe glass, jigger, citrus squeezer, shaker, strainer, peeler

Measure the gin, lemon juice, and simple syrup into an ice-filled shaker. Shake until well chilled. Strain into a coupe glass. Top with sparkling wine. Garnish with the lemon twist.

VARIATION TIP: Using the golden ratio cocktail formula (see page 23) you can easily customize the French 75 by swapping in an infused simple syrup such as the Earl Grey Syrup (page 137). You'll find the botanicals in the gin play well with the bergamot in the Earl Grey. A liqueur such as the fragrant crème de violette could also be used in place of the syrup.

Mango con Chili Bellini

Sweet, Sour

The traditional Bellini, made of white peach purée and Prosecco, was created in the 1940s by Giuseppe Cipriani, the founder of the famed Harry's Bar in Venice, Italy. The pink hue of the drink matched a garment in a painting by Venetian artist Giovanni Bellini, and Cipriani was inspired to name the drink after him. We're venturing from Italy to Mexico with this version, which swaps out the peach for mango nectar and adds lime juice, a pinch of salt, and a chili-sugar rim.

Lime wedge, for rim

¼ teaspoon chili powder, for rim

1 teaspoon sugar, for rim

2 ounces mango nectar

¼ ounce lime juice

Pinch salt

3 ounces sparkling wine

To rim a chilled coupe or champagne glass, cut a wedge of lime and swipe it around only half of the glass. Measure out the chili powder and sugar on a small plate, combine, and dip the wet half of the glass into the mixture. Measure the mango nectar, lime juice, and salt into an ice-filled shaker. Shake until well chilled. Strain into the prepared glass. Top with sparkling wine.

Tools needed: Coupe or champagne glass, paring knife, bar spoon, small plate, jigger, citrus squeezer, shaker, strainer

Blood Orange Mimosa

Sweet, Sour

What is brunch without the Mimosa? Would brunch even *exist* without this effortless combo of fresh orange juice and bubbly? It may not be a complete coincidence that brunch didn't really become a thing in the United States until the 1930s, and in 1934 the Mimosa first appeared in bartender Frank Meier's *The Artistry of Mixing Drinks*. It didn't officially take off as a brunch staple until the late 1970s, but the seed had been planted decades before. This subtle update transforms the basic Mimosa into a vivid ruby-colored beauty, perfect in the winter months when this luscious citrus fruit is in season.

2 ounces fresh blood orange juice

3 ounces sparkling wine

Blood orange twist, for garnish

Tools needed: Coupe glass, citrus squeezer, jigger, peeler

Measure the blood orange juice into a chilled coupe glass. Top with sparkling wine. Garnish with a blood orange twist.

DID YOU KNOW? Alfred Hitchcock was famously a fan of Mimosas. There was even a time when he was (falsely) credited with the invention of the drink because he loved it so much.

Negroni Sbagliato (Mistaken Negroni)

Strong, Sweet

The Negroni, a cocktail with equal parts gin, sweet vermouth, and a bitter aperitivo liqueur (most commonly Campari) has recently taken off as the "it" cocktail. With the resurgence of this bitter, spirit-forward classic, a lighter variation has resurfaced that just may appeal to a broader scope of folks. *Sbagliato* roughly translates to "messed up" or "mistaken" in Italian. This version is said to have been created when a busy bartender accidentally swapped the gin for Prosecco when making a Negroni. Sometimes mistakes are bellissima!

1 ounce Italian bitter aperitivo liqueur (such as Aperol or Campari)

1 ounce sweet vermouth

1 ounce Prosecco, or to taste

Orange twist, for garnish

Build the bitter liqueur, sweet vermouth, and Prosecco in a glass. Add ice and stir. Garnish with the orange twist.

PREP TIP: Although this is an equal-parts drink, you can absolutely play with the proportions. Some prefer to double up on the bubbly for an even lighter cocktail.

Tools needed: Rocks/old fashioned glass, jigger, bar spoon, peeler

Old Cuban

Sweet, Sour

Audrey Saunders, legendary bartender and owner of the now-shuttered Pegu Club in New York City, created this cross between a Mojito and a French 75. Saunders worked on this festive spin for a number of years. The original working title of the cocktail was El Cubano. Saunders is famous for revamping classics, but the Old Cuban is her most widely known creation and is shared worldwide.

7 mint leaves, divided

¾ ounce freshly squeezed lime juice

1½ ounces aged rum (such as Bacardi 8 Year)

1 ounce Simple Syrup (page 135)

1 or 2 dashes bitters

2 ounces sparkling wine

In a shaker, gently muddle 6 mint leaves with the lime juice. Add the rum, simple syrup, bitters, and ice. Shake until well chilled. Strain into a glass and top with sparkling wine. Garnish with the remaining mint leaf.

PREP TIP: Be sure to use a rum with a little age on it instead of a white rum: hence the name Old Cuban.

Tools needed: Nick and Nora glass, shaker, citrus squeezer, muddler, jigger, strainer

Seelbach

Strong, Sweet

Louisville, Kentucky's downtown Seelbach Hotel has always attracted a glamorous set, from F. Scott Fitzgerald to Al Capone. So it's not a surprise it would have an equally glitzy signature cocktail. The recipe of bourbon, orange liqueur, bitters, and bubbles was once believed to have been a classic unearthed in the '90s after years of obscurity. The drink's creator, bartender Adam Seger, eventually confessed to having fabricated the story in order to create buzz for the hotel.

1 ounce bourbon

½ ounce Cointreau

3 or 4 dashes Angostura bitters

3 or 4 dashes Peychaud's bitters

Sparkling wine

Orange peel, for garnish

In a chilled glass, stir together the bourbon, Cointreau, Angostura bitters, and Peychaud's bitters. Top with sparkling wine, just enough to fill the glass, and stir. Garnish with the orange peel.

Tools needed: Coupe glass, jigger, bar spoon, peeler

Twinkle

Strong, Dry

The Twinkle was created in 2002 by British bar legend Tony Conigliaro. This simple and festive cocktail contains a whopping 3 ounces of vodka and only ¾ ounce of liqueur, making for a slightly floral, yet rather dry, sparkling wine cocktail.

3 ounces vodka

¾ ounce elder-flower liqueur

Sparkling wine

Lemon twist, for garnish

Measure the vodka and elderflower liqueur into an ice-filled shaker. Shake until well chilled. Strain into a chilled Nick and Nora glass. Top with sparkling wine, just enough to fill the glass. Garnish with the lemon twist.

VARIATION TIP: This simple sparkler is an easy one to play with. You can substitute gin for the vodka, or another liqueur in place of the elderflower liqueur. Try this with a grapefruit, pear, or berry liqueur, depending on the season.

> **Tools needed:** Nick and Nora glass, jigger, shaker, strainer, peeler

CHAPTER 4
Gin

When it comes to the great cocktail revival, there is no other spirit as important as gin to help usher in a new era. In the early days of the cocktail explosion, there were entire bars devoted to gin cocktails—there still are! This *gin*aissance has created a generation of craft distillers from around the world making a variety of juniper-forward spirits. Gin's nuance and versatility make it a favorite among bartenders. Its botanicals tend to play well with many different ingredients, whether you are making a classic Martini, a bittersweet Negroni, or a refreshing Gin and Tonic.

Limoncello Gin & Tonic 54

Gin-Gin Mule 55

Ginger Bee's Knees 56

Negroni Snow Cone 57

Water Lily 59

Earl Grey MarTEAni 60

Cosmonaut 61

The Last Word 62

Bramble 63

Martini 64

Limoncello Gin & Tonic

Sweet, Sour

Gin and tonic (2 ounces gin, 4 to 6 ounces tonic water) is a match made in highball heaven. There's a reason why this combo has stayed in fashion for nearly 200 years. The fragrant botanicals in the gin alongside the tonic's bittersweet bubbles make for a deeply nuanced yet refreshing summertime sipper. This version mixes it up with the addition of limoncello and basil garnish, conjuring images of happy hour on the Amalfi Coast.

2 ounces gin

½ ounce Limoncello (page 140)

4 ounces tonic

Lemon wedge, for garnish

Basil leaf, for garnish

Measure the gin and Limoncello into an ice-filled wine glass. Top with tonic and stir. Garnish with the lemon wedge and basil.

VARIATION TIP: The Gin and Tonic highball is one of the most versatile cocktail canvases for experimentation. You can add a splash of Aperol or fortified wine and turn it into an aperitif or switch up the garnishes with different fruit and herbs.

> **Tools needed:** Stemmed wine glass, jigger, bar spoon, paring knife

Gin-Gin Mule

Strong, Sweet

Both the Moscow Mule and the Mojito were extremely popular at the onset of the cocktail revival. Audrey Saunders, owner of the Pegu Club and protégé of "King Cocktail" Dale DeGroff, created this now ubiquitous instant classic that merges these two beloved cocktails and swaps in gin as the base spirit.

6 mint sprigs, divided

¾ ounce lime juice

1 ounce Simple Syrup (page 135)

1½ ounces gin

1 ounce ginger beer

In a cocktail shaker, muddle 4 of the mint sprigs with lime juice and simple syrup. Add the gin and ice and shake until well chilled. Add the ginger beer to the shaker and stir. Strain into an ice-filled glass. Garnish with the remaining 2 mint sprigs.

DID YOU KNOW? Saunders's purpose in creating a lot of the cocktails she made in the early days of the Pegu Club was to help people get over their phobia of gin. She points to this cocktail in particular as a turning point in people's perceptions.

Tools needed: Highball/Collins glass, shaker, muddler, jigger, citrus squeezer, bar spoon, strainer

Ginger Bee's Knees

Sweet, Sour

The Bee's Knees is a simple sour cocktail from the Prohibition era, traditionally made with gin, lemon juice, and honey syrup. It is adorably named after the slang of the time that meant something or someone was highly admired. This version is close to the original, but uses Ginger Honey Syrup (page 136) for a spicy kick, adding even more complexity. The combination of ginger, lemon, and gin makes for some delicious giggle water that you'll be calling the cat's pajamas!

2 ounces gin

¾ ounce freshly squeezed lemon juice

¾ ounce Ginger Honey Syrup (page 136)

Lemon twist, for garnish

Measure the gin, lemon juice, and ginger honey syrup into an ice-filled shaker. Shake until well chilled. Strain into a chilled cocktail glass. Garnish with a lemon twist.

VARIATION TIP: If you prefer a classic Bee's Knees without the ginger, make a simple honey syrup by combining ½ cup honey and ½ cup water in a small saucepan. Stir over medium heat until the honey dissolves.

Tools needed: Coupe or Nick & Nora glass, jigger, citrus squeezer, shaker, strainer, peeler

Negroni Snow Cone

Sweet, Sour

As the worldwide obsession with the Negroni continues, so do the variations on this bittersweet favorite. The uncomplicated equal-parts ratio is the perfect canvas to plug and play different spirits. This adaptation is the original recipe in the form of an adult snow cone!

1 ounce gin

1 ounce Campari

1 ounce sweet vermouth

4 to 6 ice cubes

Filtered water

Orange twist, for garnish

Tools needed:
Wine glass, jigger, mixing glass, blender, strainer, peeler

Measure the gin, Campari, and sweet vermouth into a mixing glass and set aside. Put the ice cubes in a blender and add enough filtered water so the cubes float above the blades. Blend, gradually increasing to a high speed, until the ice is well crushed. Drain off the water and immediately scoop the ice into a wine glass. Strain the cocktail over the crushed ice. Express oils from a large orange twist into the drink, then add the twist to the glass for garnish.

PREP TIP: To make a slushy version of this, put the Negroni mixture in the blender with the crushed ice and blend together. Then pour into the glass.

Water Lily

Strong, Sour

This pale lavender concoction may resemble the classic Aviation cocktail with its gin, lemon juice, and crème de violette. However, the Water Lily is a more recent creation, invented by New York bartender Richard Boccato in honor of Georgette Moger-Petraske, when she was engaged to Sasha Petraske, owner of the legendary bar Milk & Honey. This equal-parts cocktail is strong but balanced, with the citrus complementing the floral qualities.

- ¾ ounce gin
- ¾ ounce orange liqueur (such as Cointreau)
- ¾ ounce crème de violette
- ¾ ounce freshly squeezed lemon juice
- Lemon twist, for garnish

Measure the gin, orange liqueur, crème de violette, and lemon juice into an ice-filled shaker. Shake until well chilled. Strain into a chilled glass. Express lemon oils from the twist into the drink, then discard.

DID YOU KNOW? The name of this cocktail was inspired by Georgette's middle name, Lillian. She has also said that when the ice chips float to the top of the drink, it can resemble Monet's water lilies.

Tools needed: Nick and Nora glass, jigger, citrus squeezer, shaker, strainer, peeler

Earl Grey MarTEAni

Strong, Sour

This twist on a Gin Sour is from Audrey Saunders, owner of New York's Pegu Club. The original recipe calls for an Earl Grey–infused gin. In a cocktail bar, they can infuse an entire bottle of gin and easily go through it over the course of a weekend. For this recipe, the tea flavors come from an infused simple syrup.

Lemon wedge, for rim (optional)

1 teaspoon sugar, for rim (optional)

1½ ounces gin

¾ ounce freshly squeezed lemon juice

1 ounce Earl Grey Syrup (page 137)

1 egg white

Lemon twist, for garnish

If sugaring the rim of the coupe glass, cut a slice into the lemon wedge and swipe it around only half of the glass. Measure out the sugar on a small plate and dip the wet half of the glass into it and set aside. Measure the gin, lemon juice, Earl Grey simple syrup, and egg white into a cocktail shaker without ice. Dry shake vigorously for 10 seconds. Add ice and shake once more. Strain into the glass. Garnish with the lemon twist.

> **Tools needed:** Coupe glass, paring knife, bar spoon, small plate, jigger, citrus squeezer, shaker, strainer, peeler

Cosmonaut

Sweet, Sour

This creation is from Sasha Petraske, the founder of Milk & Honey, the notable cocktail bar that helped usher in the cocktail renaissance. The Cosmonaut was so named as a cheeky nod to a popular vodka cocktail—the Cosmopolitan (page 96)—at the time of its creation. It may be closer, however, to the 1930s Marmalade Cocktail by Harry Craddock.

2 ounces gin

¾ ounce freshly squeezed lemon juice

1 heaping teaspoon raspberry preserves

Measure the gin, lemon juice, and preserves into an ice-filled shaker. Shake until well chilled. Double strain through a fine-mesh strainer into a chilled glass.

> **Tools needed:** Nick and Nora glass, jigger, citrus squeezer, bar spoon, shaker, fine-mesh strainer

The Last Word

Sweet, Sour

The Last Word is an equal-parts cocktail born at the Detroit Athletic Club around 1916. It went into relative obscurity until the recipe was dug up by Seattle bartender Murray Stenson in 2004. He discovered it in Ted Saucier's 1951 cocktail book *Bottoms Up!* (which credited the Detroit Athletic Club), and after adding it to the menu at Seattle's Zig Zag Café, word spread and a classic was reborn. Chartreuse liqueur can be pricey but is a necessary ingredient in this drink. It is also a key component in the Naked & Famous (page 87).

¾ ounce gin

¾ ounce green Chartreuse

¾ ounce maraschino liqueur

¾ ounce freshly squeezed lime juice

Brandied cherries, for garnish

Measure the gin, chartreuse, maraschino liqueur, and lime juice into an ice-filled shaker. Shake until well chilled. Strain into a chilled coupe glass. Garnish with brandied cherries.

DID YOU KNOW? Green Chartreuse also makes an appearance in the classic Bijou cocktail, a martini variation created in the late 1800s that is equal parts gin, sweet vermouth and green Chartreuse.

Tools needed: Coupe glass, jigger, citrus squeezer, shaker, strainer

Bramble

Sweet, Sour

This modernized classic cocktail was created by UK bartender Dick Bradsell in 1984 while he was at Fred's Club in London. Inspired by his childhood going blackberry picking on the Isle of Wight, off the southern coast of England, this cocktail brings together gin, lemon, and blackberry liqueur over crushed ice.

2 ounces gin

1 ounce freshly squeezed lemon juice

½ ounce Simple Syrup (page 135)

½ ounce blackberry liqueur (such as crème de mûre)

Lemon wedge, for garnish

Blackberry, for garnish

Measure the gin, lemon juice, and simple syrup into an ice-filled shaker. Shake until well chilled. Strain into a glass filled with crushed ice. Top with the blackberry liqueur. Garnish with the lemon wedge and blackberry.

VARIATION TIP: Black currant (crème de cassis) or raspberry liqueur (Chambord) can be used in place of the blackberry liqueur. For a floral, lavender-hued version, try using crème de violette as the liqueur ingredient.

Tools needed: Rocks/old fashioned glass, jigger, citrus squeezer, shaker, strainer, paring knife

Martini

Dry

The Martini is perhaps one of the most famous, if not *the* most famous cocktail out there. It's no surprise that its origin story is unclear, but what is clear is that it has gone through a considerable evolution since it first popped up in cocktail books in the 19th century. It started out on the sweeter side, with equal parts Old Tom Gin and sweet vermouth; The "Dirty Martini" emerged in the early 20th century when muddled olives and brine were a popular addition; And in the 1960s, it went through a major transformation when fictional British Secret Service agent James Bond ordered his Martini with vodka. "Shaken, not stirred" was an iconic catchphrase in Bond films for decades. That all said, everyone should know how to make a Martini as close to its traditional recipe, specs, and instructions, and then they can play with it from there.

2 ounces gin

1 ounce dry vermouth

Dash orange bitters (optional)

Lemon twist, for garnish

Measure the gin and vermouth into the mixing glass. Add the bitters and ice and stir until well chilled, for a good 30 seconds. Strain into a chilled glass. Garnish with lemon twist.

VARIATION TIP: If you prefer your Martinis with vodka, this is an easy one to change. If you like your Martinis on the dirty side, add ¼ ounce of olive brine and swap the twist for a few skewered olives. For a Gibson, garnish with a pickled onion instead.

> **Tools needed:** Coupe glass, jigger, mixing glass, bar spoon, strainer, peeler

CHAPTER 5

Rum

Born in the Caribbean in the 17th century, rum was an important ingredient used to make punch-style drinks and toddies in the 1600s, before *cocktail* was even a word. The post-Prohibition tiki explosion introduced a new style of drink, and rum was the star ingredient. In the recent cocktail resurgence, rum has been rediscovered as an adaptable spirit that works well in a variety of cocktails. It can be dry, unaged, and feature bright fruit—a perfect base for a refreshing Daiquiri. Or it can be rich and sweet, with a spicy funk, bold enough to stand up to an assortment of tropical ingredients.

Monsoon Slushy **68**	Piña Colada **73**
Mojito **69**	Jungle Bird **74**
Hemingway Daiquiri **70**	El Presidente **75**
Sarong Queen **71**	Cable Car **76**

Monsoon Slushy

Sweet, Makes 4 drinks

The Dark 'n' Stormy is a classic highball traditionally made with Gosling's Black Seal rum, spicy ginger beer, and a squeeze of lime. It's a simple mixed drink that has enjoyed consistent popularity since its creation in Bermuda in the 1800s. This frosty twist calls for any brand of robust, dark rum, a slightly larger ratio of lime juice, and crushed ice for a slushy consistency. The pinch of salt elevates the delicious combo.

¾ cup dark rum

1 (12-ounce) bottle ginger beer

2 ounces lime juice

Pinch salt

1 cup ice

4 lime wheels, for garnish

Measure the rum, ginger beer, lime juice, salt, and ice into a blender and blend until slushy. Pour into 4 glasses and garnish with the lime wheels.

DID YOU KNOW? Cocktail legend has it that the Dark 'n' Stormy was named by a sailor who remarked that the color was reminiscent of a storm cloud too dangerous to sail under.

Tools needed: Highball/Collins glasses, measuring cup, jigger, citrus squeezer, blender, paring knife

Mojito

Strong, Sweet

The basic recipe for the Mojito, a Cuban highball-style cocktail, originally came out of a need to mask the harsh flavors of crudely made rum. Lime, mint, and sugar have been used alongside a sugarcane spirit in the Caribbean for hundreds of years, and indigenous South Americans were said to have used it for medicinal and recreational purposes. Some historians credit the enslaved Africans who worked the sugarcane fields in 19th-century Cuba with the cocktail's invention. Once Prohibition hit the states and Havana became a popular boozy destination, the Mojito got a makeover with bubbly soda water and quality rum in an elegant highball glass.

7 mint leaves, divided

1 ounce freshly squeezed lime juice

½ ounce Simple Syrup (page 135)

2 ounces white rum

Club soda

Lime wheel, for garnish

In a shaker, gently muddle 6 mint leaves with the lime juice and simple syrup. Add the rum and ice and shake until well chilled. Strain into an ice-filled glass. Top with soda and stir. Garnish with the lime wheel and the remaining mint leaf.

Tools needed: Highball/Collins glass, shaker, muddler, jigger, strainer, bar spoon, paring knife

Hemingway Daiquiri

Sweet, Sour

Created in Cuba, the Daiquiri was the first classic cocktail invented and popularized outside of the United States. Ernest Hemingway fell hard for the Daiquiri at the Havana bar El Floridita. Legend has it he downed their blended version with abandon, but requested his be made with double the rum and no sugar. The bartender supposedly complied, and the drink was called the Papa Doble. Somewhere along the way, the recipe morphed back to include sugar, and it became known as the Hemingway Daiquiri.

2 ounces white rum

¾ ounce key lime juice

½ ounce grapefruit juice

½ ounce maraschino liqueur

¼ ounce Simple Syrup (page 135)

Lime wheel, for garnish (optional)

Measure the rum, lime juice, grapefruit juice, maraschino liqueur, and simple syrup into a shaker with ice. Shake until chilled. Strain into a coupe glass. Garnish with the lime wheel (if using).

VARIATION TIP: This sour is another versatile canvas for experimentation. It can be slightly altered by swapping in infused simple syrups, spices, juices, or various liqueurs.

Tools needed: Coupe glass, jigger, citrus squeezer, shaker, strainer, paring knife

Sarong Queen

Sweet

This drink is named for Dorothy Lamour, the glamorous actress who starred in the 1936 film *The Jungle Princess*. In the film, she wore an Edith Head–designed sarong that would earn her the nickname "Sarong Queen." This tropical aperitif cocktail is refreshing and bright from the white rum, lime, and bittersweet Aperol. The coconut water smooths out the flavors for an easy-drinking, summer sipper.

- 2 ounces white rum
- 2 ounces coconut water
- 1 ounce Italian bitter aperitivo liqueur (such as Aperol or Campari)
- 1 ounce freshly squeezed lime juice
- ½ ounce Orgeat Syrup (page 139)
- Pinch salt
- Lime wheel, for garnish
- Umbrella (optional)

Measure the rum, coconut water, bitter liqueur, lime juice, orgeat syrup, and salt into a shaker with ice. Shake until chilled. Strain into a glass filled with ice. Garnish with the lime wheel and an umbrella (if using).

Tools needed: Collins glass, jigger, citrus squeezer, shaker, strainer, paring knife

Piña Colada

Sweet

The Piña Colada was created in San Juan, Puerto Rico, by bartender Ramón "Monchito" Marrero in 1954. In 1978, Puerto Rico named it their national drink. The simple blend of cream of coconut, pineapple juice, and white rum made for a magical combination that has been a favorite beachside staple ever since.

2 ounces Puerto Rican white rum

1½ ounces cream of coconut (preferably Coco Lopez)

1½ ounces unsweetened pineapple juice

1 cup ice

Pineapple wedge, for garnish (optional)

Coffee beans, for garnish (optional)

Measure the rum, cream of coconut, pineapple juice, and ice into a blender and blend on high until smooth. Pour into a chilled glass and garnish with the pineapple wedge (if using) and coffee beans (if using).

VARIATION TIP: For an easy and delicious update, try adding 1 ounce of Coffee Liqueur (page 142) to the recipe. This will complement the pineapple and coconut surprisingly well, adding a nutty depth of flavor.

Tools needed: Highball or Collins glass, jigger, measuring cup, blender, paring knife

Jungle Bird

Strong, Sweet

Invented in the 1970s at the Aviary Bar in Kuala Lumpur, the Jungle Bird is a rare, tiki-style cocktail that is relatively simple to make with a manageable ingredient list. Created near the end of the tiki era, the Jungle Bird, though relatively unknown, was kept alive through various cocktail books over the years, including tiki historian Jeff "Beachbum" Berry's book. This version features a Jamaican-style rum and specs that reflect the most commonly used recipe.

1½ ounces Jamaican rum

1½ ounces pineapple juice

¾ ounce Campari

½ ounce Simple Syrup (page 135)

½ ounce lime juice

Pineapple wedge, for garnish

Measure the rum, pineapple juice, Campari, simple syrup, and lime juice into a shaker with ice. Shake until chilled. Strain into a glass filled with crushed ice. Garnish with the pineapple wedge.

DID YOU KNOW? The Jungle Bird was created as a welcome drink for guests at the Kuala Lumpur Hilton hotel and was served in a ceramic glass shaped like a bird.

Tools needed: Rocks/old fashioned glass, jigger, shaker, strainer, paring knife

El Presidente

Strong

The spirit-forward, Manhattan-style drink was created in the 1910s in a little café in Havana. It combines Bacardi rum, a spoonful of curaçao, and vermouth de Chambéry, an old-style semi-sweet blanc vermouth from the French Alps that's key to the overall cocktail. Dolin Blanc is often used for this crucial ingredient. This version of El Presidente comes from *cantinero* (bartender) and native Cuban Julio Cabrera, from Miami's Cafe La Trova, who claims to have perfected it over three decades.

- 1½ ounces blended aged rum
- ¾ ounce blanc vermouth (preferably Dolin Blanc)
- ½ ounce dry curaçao
- 1 teaspoon grenadine
- Orange peel, for garnish
- Morello cherry, for garnish

Measure the rum, vermouth, curaçao, and grenadine into a mixing glass over ice and stir until chilled. Strain into a chilled coupe glass. Express orange oils from the peel into the glass and discard. Garnish with the cherry.

PREP TIP: This version is a lighter and lower-ABV cocktail than most stirred, spirit-forward renditions. The cherry garnish takes its inspiration from the Manhattan, but this recipe can also benefit from an orange twist and orange bitters.

Tools needed: Coupe glass, jigger, bar spoon, mixing glass, peeler

Cable Car

Sweet, Sour

This spiced rum cocktail was created by bartender Tony Abou-Ganim, also known as "the Modern Mixologist," as the signature cocktail for the Starlight Room in San Francisco. Named for the cable car tracks near the bar, it takes inspiration from the 19th-century Brandy Crusta cocktail, with its sugared rim and orange curaçao.

Lemon wedge, for rim

½ teaspoon ground cinnamon, for rim

½ teaspoon sugar, for rim

1½ ounces spiced rum

1 ounce freshly squeezed lemon juice

¾ ounce orange curaçao

½ ounce Simple Syrup (page 135)

Orange twist, for garnish

To rim the glass, cut a slice into the lemon wedge and swipe it around half of the glass. Measure the cinnamon and sugar onto a small plate, dip half the glass into the mixture, and set aside. Measure the rum, lemon juice, curaçao, and simple syrup into an ice-filled shaker. Shake until well chilled. Strain into the prepared glass. Express orange oils from the twist over the glass and add the twist to the glass for garnish.

> **Tools needed:** Coupe or Nick and Nora glass, paring knife, bar spoon, small plate, jigger, shaker, strainer, peeler

CHAPTER 6
Tequila & Mezcal

Tequila and mezcal are both agave-based spirits; however, they can vary greatly in taste and style. They're made with different types of agave plants and in different regions of Mexico, and both spirits have their own distinctive distilling methods. There are particularly strict regulations around tequila production. For mezcal, the process of roasting the heart of the agave plant in earthen pits in the ground for multiple days tends to give it a characteristic smoky quality that lends itself well to sweet and savory cocktails alike. Both tequila and mezcal are complex spirits that range from fresh and vegetal to honeyed and earthy, making for surprising versatility in a variety of cocktails, from a spicy Margarita to a Oaxaca Old Fashioned.

Ranch Water 80	The Veracruz 86
Brighton Beachcomber 81	Naked & Famous 87
Jalapeño Cucumber Margarita 83	Oaxaca Old Fashioned 88
Mezcal Paloma 85	Tía Mía 89

Ranch Water

Dry

This refreshing tequila highball is the unofficial cocktail of West Texas. The exact origins are uncertain and highly contested, with some claiming it actually has roots as a traditional Mexican drink. There is no disputing, however, the refreshing and simple beauty of this sessionable (i.e., low-alcohol) warm-weather cocktail. Topo Chico is a favorite soda water to use here because of its distinctly small bubbles.

2 ounces blanco tequila

½ ounce freshly squeezed lime juice

4 or 5 dashes grapefruit bitters

Soda water

Grapefruit twist, for garnish

In a highball glass, build the drink by adding the tequila, lime juice, and bitters. Add ice, top with soda water, and stir. Express grapefruit oils from the twist over the glass and add the twist to the glass for garnish.

VARIATION TIP: Reposado or añejo tequila, or even mezcal, can be used in place of the blanco tequila. Change up the bitters (try cherry or rhubarb) for a subtle difference. Add a splash of fruit liqueur or salt to the glass to make your own modifications.

Tools needed: Highball/Collins glass, jigger, bar spoon, peeler

Brighton Beachcomber

Sweet, Sour

I love using coconut water in cocktails. The flavor is pretty innocuous mixed into a drink, adding just a slightly sweet, nutty character. It has a clarified milk quality with a luscious mouthfeel and helps to smooth out the edges in a cocktail, especially with powerful ingredients like tequila, lime, and ginger. This drink, with its muddled cucumber and easy drinkability, evokes a summery Margarita with a soft-focus filter.

5 thin slices cucumber, divided

2 ounces blanco tequila

2 ounces coconut water

1 ounce ginger liqueur

1 ounce freshly squeezed lime juice

In a shaker, muddle 3 slices of cucumber. Measure the tequila, coconut water, ginger liqueur, lime juice, and ice into the shaker. Shake until well chilled. Strain into a chilled glass. Garnish with the remaining 2 cucumber slices floating on top.

Tools needed: Coupe glass, shaker, muddler, paring knife, jigger, strainer

TEQUILA & MEZCAL

Jalapeño Cucumber Margarita

Sweet, Sour

The Margarita, Mexico's original tequila sour, has been one of the most popular cocktails for decades. Like many classic cocktails, its origins are fuzzy. What we do know is *margarita* is Spanish for "daisy," the name of another classic sour cocktail that has been around since the late 1800s, originally made with orange cordial and a splash of soda. While the world's most beloved sour has gone through a lot of incarnations over the years, the interest in crafting new variations doesn't seem to wane. The "spicy" Margarita has been a favorite for a number of years. In this version, the peppers lend the heat and the cucumbers an opposing cooling quality. To make a traditional Margarita, simply omit the cucumber and jalapeño.

- Lime wedge, for rim
- Coarse salt, for rim
- 4 cucumber slices, divided
- 2 thin slices jalapeño pepper, seeded
- 2 ounces tequila
- 1 ounce lime juice
- ½ ounce Cointreau (or another orange liqueur)
- ½ ounce agave syrup or Simple Syrup (page 135)

CONTINUED ▶

Jalapeño Cucumber Margarita CONTINUED

Cut a slice into the lime wedge and swipe it around the rim of the glass. Put salt on a small plate and dip the rim of the glass into it. Set aside. In a shaker, gently muddle 3 cucumber slices and the jalapeño. Add the tequila, lime juice, Cointreau, and syrup and fill with ice. Shake until well chilled. Double strain into the prepared glass. Garnish with the remaining slice of cucumber.

VARIATION TIP: The Margarita continues to be an inspirational base recipe for mixologists and home bartenders alike. Swap out the orange liqueur for an elderflower or grapefruit liqueur. Turn the drink into a lighter highball or daisy by adding club soda. Swap in other fruits and herbs to add your own twist.

> **Tools needed:** Rocks/old fashioned glass, paring knife, small plate, shaker, muddler, jigger, strainer

Mezcal Paloma

Sweet, Sour

A traditional Paloma is an uncomplicated highball commonly made with tequila, grapefruit soda, lime juice, and a dash of salt. It has gone through many craft cocktail transformations this last decade, most often involving fresh grapefruit juice, liqueurs, or syrups. This recipe is in the traditional style but with a mezcal swap.

2 ounces mezcal

½ ounce freshly squeezed lime juice

Pinch salt

Grapefruit soda

Grapefruit wedge, for garnish

Measure the mezcal, lime juice, and salt into a glass. Add ice, top with grapefruit soda, and stir well to dissolve the salt. Garnish with the grapefruit wedge.

PREP TIP: If you don't like the idea of using grapefruit soda, you can opt to use 2 ounces fresh grapefruit juice, 1 ounce club soda, and ½ ounce agave nectar instead.

> **Tools needed:** Highball/Collins glass, jigger, bar spoon, paring knife

The Veracruz

Sweet, Sour

This cocktail recipe was inspired by how the tequila shots are served at the Afro-Latin bar and nightclub Bembé in Brooklyn. An order of tequila shots is accompanied by wedges of lime and two separate bowls of finely ground coffee and sugar. The lime wedge gets a coating of the coffee and sugar mixture, the tequila is shot, and then both are enjoyed together The Veracruz takes the flavor profile even further with the addition of ginger for a little heat in this bright and balanced cocktail.

2 ounces tequila

1 ounce Ginger Syrup (page 136)

1 ounce Coffee Liqueur (page 142)

1 ounce freshly squeezed lime juice

½ teaspoon ground coffee

½ teaspoon sugar

Lime wedge, for garnish

Measure the tequila, ginger syrup, coffee liqueur, and lime juice into an ice-filled shaker. Shake until well chilled. Strain into the glass. On a small plate, combine the coffee and sugar. Cut a slice into the lime wedge, dip it into the coffee and sugar mixture, and garnish the glass.

PREP TIP: The syrup and liqueur can be switched in this cocktail. Swap a ginger liqueur for the ginger syrup and a coffee syrup for the coffee liqueur for a slightly different flavor profile.

Tools needed: Coupe or Nick and Nora glass, jigger, shaker, strainer, bar spoon, small plate, paring knife

Naked & Famous

Strong, Sour

This mid-aughts creation, a favorite of craft bartenders and cocktail enthusiasts alike, was dreamed up in 2011 by Joaquín Simó while bartending at New York's Death & Co. Using dominant ingredients in equal parts, such as in the Negroni or The Last Word (page 62) can complement and balance out each bold flavor. The result is a bright, herbaceous, spirit-forward drink with a hint of smoke.

- ¾ ounce mezcal
- ¾ ounce Chartreuse (yellow or green)
- ¾ ounce Aperol
- ¾ ounce freshly squeezed lime juice

Tools needed: Coupe glass, jigger, citrus squeezer, shaker, straine

Measure the mezcal, Chartreuse, Aperol, and lime juice into an ice-filled shaker. Shake until chilled. Strain into a chilled glass.

PREP TIP: Because there is very little mezcal in this, and the other ingredients are equally bold, Simó recommends a big, smoky mezcal like Del Maguey's Chichicapa. Green Chartreuse is usually easier to find than the yellow version. While the original recipe was created with yellow Chartreuse—which is milder and slighter sweeter than green Chartreuse—the bolder and higher-alcohol sister expression can be used in its place.

Oaxaca Old Fashioned

Strong

This agave-based twist on the classic Old Fashioned was created by bartender Phil Ward while working at Death & Co in New York City. It then went on to become a cult favorite while on the menu at the now-closed Mayahuel, a tequila and mezcal bar that introduced drinkers to the versatility of agave spirits. This cocktail, which combines a reposado tequila with the rich smoke of mezcal, popularized the use of mezcal as a cocktail ingredient.

1½ ounces reposado tequila

½ ounce mezcal

1 teaspoon agave nectar

2 dashes aromatic bitters (such as Angostura)

Flamed orange peel, for garnish

Measure the tequila, mezcal, agave nectar, and bitters into a glass with a large ice cube. Stir well until chilled. Flame the orange peel over the glass (see page 21) and add to the drink.

PREP TIP: Change up the flavor by swapping out the aromatic bitters for chocolate or spicy bitters, instead.

Tools needed: Rocks/old fashioned glass, jigger, bar spoon, strainer, peeler, match

Tía Mía

Strong, Sour

This smoky mezcal take on a Mai Tai was the creation of New York bartender Ivy Mix while she was working at Julie Reiner's short-lived, Hawaiian-themed restaurant Lani Kai. As a mezcal enthusiast, and a fan of this tiki classic, she merged her favorites to create this drink, an anagram of Mai Tai, and now a regular on the menu at Mix and Reiner's bar, Leyenda, in Brooklyn.

1 ounce mezcal

1 ounce rum

¾ ounce freshly squeezed lime juice

½ ounce Orgeat Syrup (page 139)

½ ounce orange curaçao

¼ ounce Simple Syrup (page 135)

Mint sprig, for garnish

Lime wheel, for garnish

Measure the mezcal, rum, lime juice, orgeat syrup, orange curaçao, and simple syrup into a shaker with ice. Shake until chilled. Strain into a glass filled with crushed ice. Garnish with the mint sprig, and lime wheel.

PREP TIP: Try a Jamaican-style rum for added depth of flavor. And for the orange curaçao, try the brand Pierre Ferrand Dry. This cocktail can benefit from a little salt on the rim as well.

Tools needed: Rocks/old fashioned glass, jigger, shaker, strainer, paring knife

CHAPTER 7
Vodka

Vodka, as a distilled spirit, has been enjoyed in parts of the world for at least 600 years. However, as a cocktail ingredient, it didn't really catch on until the 1950s. The Moscow Mule, the Bloody Mary, and James Bond's Vodka Martini helped popularize vodka as a go-to cocktail ingredient. By the 1970s, it overtook gin and whiskey as the top-selling spirit in America. Because of its massive popularity, relative youth in cocktail culture, and its natural neutrality, vodka was viewed as an uninteresting, characterless spirit by some. Soon people realized that drinks like the Cosmopolitan and the Lemon Drop made with fresh citrus were gateway craft cocktails to the more complex, pre-Prohibition gin cocktails that were still waiting to be discovered. Vodka's neutral quality also makes it one of the most versatile base spirits, and a conduit and magnifier of flavors.

Basil Gimlet **92**

Porn Star Martini **93**

Bloody Mary **95**

Cosmopolitan **96**

Harvey Wallbanger Slushy **98**

Espresso Martini **99**

Limoncello Drop **100**

Improved Midori Sour **102**

Flatiron Martini **103**

Amelia **104**

The Fabergé (A White Russian Egg Cream) **105**

Basil Gimlet

Sweet, Sour

In 1922 the Gimlet recipe first appeared in Harry MacElhone's *Harry's ABC of Mixing Cocktails* as an equal-parts cocktail of gin and Rose's lime juice. Along the way, the sweet cordial got pushed aside in favor of fresh lime juice and handmade syrups. The Basil Gimlet, made with gin or vodka, rose in popularity in the mid-aughts and is still one you see on menus. The tart lime and aromatic basil is delightfully refreshing.

5 basil leaves, divided

2 lime wedges

2 ounces vodka

¾ ounce freshly squeezed lime juice

¾ ounce Simple Syrup (page 135)

In a shaker, gently muddle 4 basil leaves and the lime wedges. Add the vodka, lime juice, simple syrup, and ice. Shake until well chilled. Double strain into a chilled glass. Garnish with the remaining basil leaf.

VARIATION TIP: Gin can be substituted for vodka in this recipe to make a traditional gimlet. For an even lighter take, you can use the Japanese spirit shōchū in place of the vodka. The basil can be swapped for mint or another fresh herb.

Tools needed: Coupe glass, shaker, muddler, paring knife, jigger, fine-mesh strainer

Porn Star Martini

Sweet, Strong

Coming out of London's cocktail renaissance in 2003, this martini is traditionally served with a sidecar shot of sparkling wine. Douglas Ankrah created this drink, which originally included vanilla vodka and Passoã. This recipe is a simplified and slightly dry version. Ankrah called it the Porn Star Martini because he thought it was something that a porn star would drink: "It's pure indulgence, sexy, fun, and evocative."

2 ounces vodka

1 ounce passion fruit purée

1 ounce Simple Syrup (page 135)

½ ounce freshly squeezed lime juice

2 or 3 dashes vanilla extract

Passion fruit slices, for garnish (optional)

1 shot sparkling wine (optional)

Measure the vodka, passion fruit purée, simple syrup, lime juice, and vanilla into an ice-filled shaker. Shake until well chilled. Strain into a glass. Garnish with fresh passion fruit (if using). Serve with a shot of sparkling wine (if using).

PREP TIP: Passion fruit purée (or pulp) can be found in most grocery stores. If you decide to add passion fruit liqueur in addition to the passion fruit purée, reduce the simple syrup to ½ ounce and add ½ ounce of passion fruit liqueur, preferably Passoã.

Tools needed: Coupe glass, jigger, shaker, strainer, paring knife, shot glass (optional)

VODKA

Bloody Mary

Dry

As with most classics, the origin of the Bloody Mary is unclear. The most credible story is that it was created by a bartender named Fernand "Pete" Petiot in the early 1920s while he was working in Paris at Harry's New York Bar. He brought it back to the states with him after Prohibition, and a brunch-time staple had arrived! If you're a Bloody Mary fan, you may already have your own go-to tricks to spice up this savory favorite.

- 2 ounces vodka
- 4 ounces Bloody Mary Mix (page 141)
- ¼ ounce freshly squeezed lemon juice
- 1 celery stalk, for garnish
- Lemon wedge, for garnish
- Olives, for garnish

Measure the vodka, Bloody Mary mix, and lemon juice into a highball glass with ice. Pour the mixture 3 or 4 times back and forth into a mixing glass to mix well. Garnish with the celery stalk, lemon wedge, and skewered olives.

PREP TIP: The Bloody Mary is made for experimentation. Like more salt or spice in your mix? Want to up the citrus or take it out entirely? Enjoy garnishes like bacon or cheese in your drink? Go to town!

Tools needed: Highball/Collins glass, jigger, mixing glass, paring knife, cocktail pick

Cosmopolitan

Sweet, Sour

This cocktail made a name for itself in the TV series *Sex and the City*, but the drink had been making the rounds in the *real* New York City for a number of years before that. Toby Cecchini, the bartender credited with the creation of the Cosmo, came up with this drink in 1988 while behind the bar at the Odeon. The drink was inspired by another drink of the same name: a combination of vodka, Rose's lime juice, and grenadine. Cecchini swapped the Rose's for fresh lime juice and built the drink as a traditional sour with a 2:1:1:1 ratio. Absolut Citron vodka was a hot new brand when the drink was created and served as the base spirit, but it can be exchanged with another citrus or unflavored vodka. This version is a paler, more blush-colored version than you may have seen elsewhere, but these are the original specs from the man who invented it. When you stick to this ratio, you'll understand why the Cosmo is an instant favorite.

2 ounces Absolut Citron vodka

1 ounce Cointreau

1 ounce cranberry juice

1 ounce freshly squeezed lime juice

Lemon twist, for garnish

Measure the vodka, Cointreau, cranberry juice, and lime juice into a shaker with ice. Shake until cold to the touch. Strain into a chilled glass. Express lemon oils from the twist, rub it against the rim of the glass, and drop it in.

PREP TIP: A lemon twist is traditional in the Cosmo. However, famed bartender Dale DeGroff, also known as "King Cocktail," made his version with a flamed orange peel. A grapefruit twist can also work well in this drink.

Tools needed: Coupe or martini glass, jigger, shaker, strainer, peeler

Harvey Wallbanger Slushy

Sweet, Sour, Makes 4 drinks

Though the Harvey Wallbanger was created in the 1950s, it took about two more decades for it to really take off. In the golden days of 1970s disco, this drink was huge. It disappeared from the cocktail lexicon for a few decades, but the new era of craft cocktails has come to embrace it again. The simple recipe is a screwdriver—orange juice and vodka—with the addition of the Italian liqueur Galliano floated on top (see page 4 for this technique). This slushy version transforms a breakfast cocktail into an after-dinner treat.

1 cup vodka

2 ounces Galliano

2 ounces freshly squeezed lemon juice

1½ cups orange sorbet

1 cup ice

Orange slice, for garnish

Maraschino cherry, for garnish

In a blender, combine the vodka, Galliano, lemon juice, sorbet, and ice, and blend until slushy. Pour into highball glasses and garnish with a skewered orange slice and maraschino cherry.

PREP TIP: If you want to do the Galliano "floater," top each drink with an additional ¼ ounce of Galliano.

> **Tools needed:** Highball/Collins glasses, blender, jigger, measuring cup, paring knife, cocktail pick

Espresso Martini

Sweet, Strong

The Espresso Martini is the stuff of legends. Created in 1983 by Dick Bradsell at London's Soho Brasserie, a famous model (rumored to be Kate Moss) requested a drink that would "wake me up, and then f**k me up." The espresso station was next to the bar, and a beloved drink came together. This recipe includes a pinch of salt and a touch of lemon to help highlight the smoke, fruit, and nutty flavors.

- 2 ounces vodka
- 1 ounce freshly brewed espresso
- 1 ounce Coffee Liqueur (page 142)
- Pinch salt
- Lemon twist, for garnish
- Coffee beans, for garnish

Measure the vodka, espresso, coffee liqueur, and salt into an ice-filled shaker. Shake until well chilled. Strain into a chilled glass. Express lemon oils from the twist into the glass and discard. Garnish with coffee beans.

PREP TIP: To get an extra frothy top for your Espresso Martini, make sure to shake this one for an extra-long time. If you don't have access to fresh espresso at home, you can substitute strong, freshly brewed regular coffee, cooled. If this recipe isn't sweet enough, try adding ¼ or ½ ounce of simple syrup.

Tools needed: Nick and Nora or coupe glass, jigger, shaker, strainer, peeler

Limoncello Drop

Sweet, Sour

The Lemon Drop, a straightforward vodka-based sour, is one of the few cocktails to come out of the 1970s intact. The candy-inspired drink was created by Norman Jay Hobday, the owner of Henry Africa's bar in San Francisco, the very first "fern bar" (or singles bar) in the country, in order to please the palates of the many women frequenting the place. Little did he know that he would create a singles bar revolution and an iconic cocktail both men and women would enjoy for decades. This drink adjusts the original formula to include our handmade Limoncello (page 140) for a deeper flavor profile and a richer citrus punch.

- Lemon wedge, for rim
- Superfine sugar, for rim
- 1 ounce vodka
- 1 ounce Limoncello (page 140)
- 1 ounce freshly squeezed lemon juice
- ½ ounce Grand Marnier
- Lemon twist, for garnish

Cut a slice into the lemon wedge and swipe it around the top of a chilled coupe glass. Pour some sugar onto a small plate, dip the glass into the sugar, and set aside. Measure the vodka, limoncello, lemon juice, and Grand Marnier into a shaker with ice. Shake until well chilled. Strain into the prepared glass. Garnish with the lemon twist.

VARIATION TIP: To make a classic Lemon Drop, use 2 ounces vodka, ½ ounce Grand Marnier (or another orange liqueur), 1 ounce lemon juice, and 1 ounce Simple Syrup (page 135). This cocktail can also easily be transformed into a Sparkling Limoncello Drop. Opt for a larger glass, and after straining the cocktail from the shaker, top with 1 to 2 ounces of sparkling wine.

Tools needed: Coupe glass, paring knife, small plate, jigger, shaker, strainer, peeler

Improved Midori Sour

Sweet, Sour

If you thought you knew the Midori Sour, the 1970s Day-Glo ode to disco and candy-flavored cocktails, take another look! Back then, the melon-flavored Midori liqueur was often covered up with sugar-laden sour mix and zero fresh citrus. In this revised version, the delicate melon qualities are highlighted with the addition of fresh lime juice. The egg white adds a creamy mouthfeel, while the splash of soda lightens up the overall drink.

1 ounce Midori liqueur

1 ounce vodka

1 ounce freshly squeezed lime juice

1 egg white

Club soda

Lime wheel, for garnish

Measure the Midori, vodka, lime juice, and egg white into a shaker. Dry shake for 10 to 15 seconds. Add ice and shake again. Strain into an ice-filled glass. Top with soda and garnish with the lime wheel.

DID YOU KNOW? Midori liqueur made its American debut at Studio 54 in New York City at a launch party for *Saturday Night Fever*, where the cast and crew sipped on Midori-fueled "Japanese Gin & Tonics."

Tools needed: Highball/Collins glass, jigger, shaker, strainer, paring knife

Flatiron Martini

Strong, Dry

This Vodka Martini variation was a favorite at the now-closed Flatiron Lounge in New York City. Bartender and owner Julie Reiner created this elegant riff that became a constant on the menu. The Cointreau rinse and Lillet Blanc create a slightly fruity and floral martini, but still on the dry side.

Cointreau, for rinse

1½ ounces vodka

1½ ounces Lillet Blanc

Orange twist, for garnish

Rinse the glass with Cointreau until it's well coated on the inside. Discard excess liqueur, and set the glass aside. Measure the vodka and Lillet into an ice-filled mixing glass. Stir until well chilled. Strain into the prepared glass. Garnish with the orange twist.

PREP TIP: Some recipes call for an orange-flavored vodka such as Grey Goose L'Orange. Using a quality, citrus-flavored vodka will add some dimension and help to highlight the Cointreau and the orange peels in the Lillet Blanc.

Tools needed: Coupe or Nick and Nora glass, jigger, mixing glass, bar spoon, strainer, peeler

Amelia

Strong, Sour

For over 15 years, this cocktail has been one of the most popular at famed cocktail den Employees Only in New York City. The combination of lush blackberries, elderflower liqueur, and mint creates a heady sipper that goes down very easily. Created by EO founders and proprietors Jason Kosmas and Dushan Zaric, this drink is fruit-forward but balanced, and not too sweet.

4 blackberries

¾ ounce freshly squeezed lemon juice

2 ounces vodka

1 ounce elderflower liqueur

Fresh mint, for garnish

In a shaker, gently muddle the blackberries with the lemon juice. Add the vodka, elderflower liqueur, and ice and shake until chilled. Double-strain into a chilled glass. Spank mint in the palm of your hand to release the aromatic oils and use it to garnish the glass.

Tools needed: Nick and Nora glass, shaker, muddler, citrus squeezer, jigger, fine-mesh strainer

The Fabergé (A White Russian Egg Cream)

Sweet

This cocktail is the result of a mash-up between a White Russian and an egg cream, hence the name: The Fabergé. This recipe benefits from a good-quality Coffee Liqueur (page 142) and chocolate syrup.

2 ounces vodka

1 ounce Coffee Liqueur (page 142)

½ ounce half-and-half

½ ounce chocolate syrup

Club soda

Measure the vodka, coffee liqueur, half-and-half, and chocolate syrup into an ice-filled shaker. Shake until well chilled. Strain into a glass filled with ice. Top with soda and stir.

Tools needed: Highball/Collins glass, jigger, shaker, strainer, bar spoon

CHAPTER 8
Whisk(e)y

When we think of the beginnings of cocktail culture, whiskey cocktails come to mind. However, in the early days of cocktail creation, brandy and rum were the mixing spirits of choice. Cognac was the dominant spirit in cocktails until the 1880s, when phylloxera, a microscopic pest with a penchant for destroying grapevines, infested Europe's vineyards and halted French wine and brandy production. Whiskey rose to take cognac's place, and during the "classics age" (1885 to 1920), whiskey, along with gin, became the preferred base spirit in cocktails. Prohibition and the years following proved a challenging time for the American whiskey industry, and quality was greatly diminished. But with the craft spirits boom coinciding with the craft cocktail revolution, whiskey once again became a favorite in mixed drinks.

- Penicillin 108
- Trinidad Sour 109
- Whiskey Cardinale 110
- Bourbon Renewal 111
- The Retox 112
- Paper Plane 113
- Coffee Old Fashioned 115
- Manhattan 116
- Vieux Carré 117
- Amore Mio 118

Penicillin

Sweet, Sour

This smoky, honeyed ginger take on a Whiskey Sour was created by Sam Ross while bartending at Milk & Honey in New York City in 2005. Inspired by their house-made ginger juice and an early shipment of peated scotch, Ross came up with a 21st-century classic. The combination of honey, ginger, lemon, and whiskey mimicked an age-old, at-home cold remedy, with an additional medicinal kick from the Islay scotch float on top (see page 4 for this technique).

2 ounces blended scotch

¾ ounce Honey Ginger Syrup (page 136)

¾ ounce freshly squeezed lemon juice

¾ ounce Islay single malt scotch

Candied ginger, for garnish

Measure the blended scotch, honey ginger syrup, and lemon juice into an ice-filled shaker. Shake until well chilled. Strain into a glass filled with one or two large ice cubes. Add the Islay single malt scotch to float on top of the drink. Garnish with candied ginger.

DID YOU KNOW? The Penicillin's popularity quickly spread when Sam Ross worked as a bar consultant in Los Angeles a few years after its invention.

Tools needed: Rocks/old fashioned glass, jigger, shaker, strainer

Trinidad Sour

Strong, Sour

This unusual cocktail, with a base of Angostura bitters, was created by bartender Giuseppe González while at Brooklyn's Clover Club in 2008. With only a half-ounce of whiskey, this recipe seems to be flipped on its head, but the intensity of the bitters is balanced out with rich orgeat and bright citrus.

- 1½ ounces Angostura bitters
- 1 ounce Orgeat Syrup (page 139)
- ¾ ounce freshly squeezed lemon juice
- ½ ounce rye whiskey

Measure the bitters, orgeat syrup, lemon juice, and whiskey into a shaker and fill with ice. Shake until well chilled. Strain into a chilled glass.

PREP TIP: To match the bold Angostura bitters, choose an overproof rye whiskey with a full body, preferably 100 proof. To soften the overall flavors, and for a frothy top, add an egg white; dry shake it with the other ingredients before adding the ice for a second shake.

> **Tools needed:** Nick and Nora glass, jigger, shaker, strainer

Whiskey Cardinale

Sweet, Sour

Named after Claudia Cardinale, the fiery Italian Tunisian movie star who rose to fame in Spaghetti Westerns of the 1960s, this exotic combination of Italian bitter liqueur, spicy rye whiskey, maple syrup, and coconut water makes for a drink that is at once complex, approachable, and surprisingly refreshing.

2 ounces rye whiskey

2 ounces coconut water

½ ounce freshly squeezed lemon juice

½ ounce Meletti Amaro

½ ounce maple syrup

Measure the whiskey, coconut water, lemon juice, amaro, and maple syrup into an ice-filled shaker. Shake until well chilled. Strain into a glass.

DID YOU KNOW? Amaro is generally served as an aperitif or digestif in Italy; however, it is a lovely modifier in cocktails, and a perfect companion to whiskey. Each amaro has its own distinctive flavor profile, and a cocktail recipe should call for a specific brand, as it can greatly affect the end result.

Tools needed: Coupe glass, jigger, shaker, strainer

Bourbon Renewal

Strong

This drink, one of the most popular orders at Clyde Common in Portland, Oregon, was created by bartender and drinks writer Jeffrey Morgenthaler. He thought the name of his friend's band was so clever that he commemorated it with this cocktail. The sweet, black currant liqueur crème de cassis adds a rich complexity, while the full ounce of lemon juice balances and brightens this springtime whiskey cocktail.

2 ounces bourbon

1 ounce freshly squeezed lemon juice

½ ounce crème de cassis

½ ounce Simple Syrup (page 135)

1 dash Angostura bitters

Lemon wedge, for garnish

Fresh currants, for garnish (optional)

Measure the bourbon, lemon juice, crème de cassis, simple syrup, and bitters into a shaker with ice. Shake until well chilled. Strain into an ice-filled glass. Garnish with a lemon wedge and fresh currants (if using).

Tools needed: Rocks/old fashioned glass, jigger, shaker, strainer, paring knife

The Retox

Strong, Sour

In 2006, Beyoncé famously shed 20 pounds in 2 weeks for her role in *Dreamgirls*. Her extreme juice diet, called the Master Cleanse, consisted of maple syrup, lemon juice, cayenne pepper, and water. It was suddenly the diet of the moment and subsequently, every bartender in the country was making their own boozy riff on it. This anti-detox includes bourbon and hard cider, obvious companions to the maple syrup, lemon, and cayenne.

2 ounces bourbon

½ ounce freshly squeezed lemon juice

½ ounce maple syrup

Pinch cayenne pepper

2 or 3 ounces hard apple cider

Lemon wheel, for garnish

Measure the bourbon, lemon juice, maple syrup, and cayenne pepper into a shaker with ice. Shake until well chilled. Strain into a glass filled with ice, and top with hard apple cider. Garnish with a lemon wheel.

Tools needed: Rocks/old fashioned glass, jigger, shaker, strainer, paring knife

Paper Plane

Strong, Sour

This equal-parts cocktail is named after the M.I.A. song that was playing on repeat in the summer of 2007, a favorite of Milk & Honey's Sasha Petraske. The drink was created by Sam Ross and Petraske for former colleague Toby Maloney's Chicago bar The Violet Hour. A riff on The Last Word (page 62), also a shaken, equal-parts cocktail with citrus, Ross included his favorite amaro at the time.

¾ ounce bourbon

¾ ounce Aperol

¾ ounce Amaro Nonino

¾ ounce freshly squeezed lemon juice

Measure the bourbon, Aperol, amaro, and lemon juice into an ice-filled shaker. Shake until well chilled. Strain into a chilled glass.

VARIATION TIP: Try substituting tequila for the bourbon and lime for the lemon to mix up this equal-parts cocktail.

Tools needed: Coupe glass, jigger, shaker, strainer

Coffee Old Fashioned

Strong

The first published definition of the word *cocktail* in 1806—"a stimulating liquor, composed of spirits of any kind, sugar, water, and bitters"—sounds remarkably like the most famous whiskey cocktail, the Old Fashioned. This drink was created at a time when the base spirit could also be brandy or Holland gin. However, whiskey was the spirit that stuck. After prohibition, the recipe went through a metamorphosis through the years, from old, stodgy fruit cup in a glass, back to the refined classic recipe. This variation uses a coffee liqueur as the sweet element, a rich and complex complement to a spicy rye whiskey.

2 ounces rye whiskey

½ ounce Coffee Liqueur (page 142)

3 or 4 dashes orange bitters

Orange peel, for garnish

Tools needed: Rocks/old fashioned glass, jigger, bar spoon, peeler

Measure the whiskey, coffee liqueur, and orange bitters into a glass with large ice cubes. Stir until mixed and well chilled. Express orange oils from the peel over the glass, then add the peel as garnish.

VARIATION TIP: The Old Fashioned recipe is by nature open to experimentation. Swap out the base spirit for a rum or brandy. Or try a split-base spirit with bourbon and brandy. Or use another liqueur to change up the flavor profile.

Manhattan

Strong

In the late 1800s, Italian (sweet) vermouth became increasingly popular with bartenders, and while we can't pinpoint exactly where the Manhattan originated, we can toast to the winning combination of American whiskey, sweet vermouth, and aromatic bitters. While I prefer the classic 2:1 specs with a nice, spicy rye whiskey, this can absolutely be made with a quality bourbon and adjusted to your taste.

2 ounces rye whiskey

1 ounce sweet vermouth

3 or 4 dashes of aromatic bitters

Brandied cherries, for garnish

Fill a mixing glass with ice along with the measured whiskey, vermouth, and bitters. Stir until well chilled. Strain into a chilled glass. Garnish with brandied cherries.

VARIATION TIP: For a "Perfect Manhattan," split the sweet vermouth with a dry vermouth, using a ½ ounce of each. For a heavier and slightly more herbaceous version, try the "Black Manhattan" by replacing the sweet vermouth with Averna amaro and add a few dashes of orange bitters.

Tools needed: Coupe glass, mixing glass, jigger, bar spoon, strainer

Vieux Carré

Strong

The Vieux Carré, which translates to "Old Square," is named after the French Quarter in New Orleans, where it was invented. In 1938, Walter Bergeron, head bartender at the Hotel Monteleone, famous for its rotating Carousel Bar, created this boozy mix of whiskey, brandy, sweet vermouth, and the herbal liqueur Bénédictine. Since it is still relatively under the radar outside of New Orleans, the recipe is left intact so you get the full experience of this iconic cocktail.

- 1 ounce rye whiskey
- 1 ounce brandy
- 1 ounce sweet vermouth
- ¼ ounce Bénédictine
- 4 dashes bitters
- Lemon twist, for garnish

Measure the whiskey, brandy, sweet vermouth, Bénédictine, and bitters into a mixing glass and fill with ice. Stir until well chilled. Strain into a rocks glass with one or two large ice cubes. Express lemon oils from the twist into the drink and add the twist to the glass.

DID YOU KNOW? Truman Capote claimed to have been born in the Hotel Monteleone, also the birthplace of the Vieux Carré cocktail.

Tools needed: Rocks/old fashioned glass, jigger, mixing glass, bar spoon, strainer, peeler

Amore Mio

Strong, Sweet

This drink, which means "my love" in Italian, was created as a Valentine's Day-inspired cocktail. It's another equal-parts cocktail in the spirit of a java-fueled Boulevardier. The three bold ingredients create a complexity of flavors. The bittersweet, candied orange in the Aperol, the earthy coffee liqueur, and the caramel and vanilla notes in the bourbon balance one another for a robust, spirit-forward drink.

1 ounce bourbon

1 ounce Coffee Liqueur (page 142)

1 ounce Aperol

3 or 4 coffee beans, for garnish

Fill a mixing glass with ice and the bourbon, coffee liqueur, and Aperol. Stir until well chilled. Strain into a chilled glass. Garnish by floating coffee beans on top.

PREP TIP: As with any equal-parts cocktail, you can play with different ratios, depending on your preference. You may want to double up the bourbon or pull back on the coffee liqueur for a more whiskey-forward drink. This drink can also be served over ice in an old fashioned glass for more dilution.

Tools needed: Coupe glass, mixing glass, jigger, bar spoon, strainer

CHAPTER 9

Wild Cards & Mixed Spirits

No matter how much of a novice you are at mixing drinks, most people have an *idea* of what to do with a bottle of whiskey or gin. Easy highball mixers like ginger ale or tonic often take the guesswork out of a quick mixed drink. But what do you do with a bottle that's not as familiar? How do you mix sherry into cocktails? What kinds of flavors go well with sake? Can a flavored liqueur be the base spirit in a cocktail? What even is cachaça?! For those more "exotic" bottles you may have received as a gift, purchased for yourself out of curiosity, or have left over from that one drink you learned to make with it, you'll soon find that you can use them very much in the same way you would any of your other favorites.

Amaretto Sour 122	**Sake Lychee Martini** 127
Caipirinha 123	**Chilcano** 128
Frosé 125	**The Adonis** 129
Grasshopper 126	**Yuzu Sour** 130

Amaretto Sour

Sweet, Sour

The original recipe of this sweet cocktail from the 1970s was nothing but sweet almond liqueur and the Day-Glo yellow-green mixture. Portland bartender Jeffrey Morgenthaler changed the Amaretto Sour cocktail game in 2012. His version includes fresh lemon juice, cask-proof bourbon, and an egg white for a creamy mouthfeel. For the cask-proof bourbon, the higher the strength, the better.

1½ ounces amaretto

¾ ounce cask-proof bourbon

1 ounce freshly squeezed lemon juice

1 teaspoon Simple Syrup (page 135)

½ ounce egg white

Lemon peel, for garnish

Brandied cherries, for garnish

Measure the amaretto, bourbon, lemon juice, simple syrup, and egg white into a shaker and dry shake without ice. Add ice and shake again until well chilled. Strain into an ice-filled glass. Garnish with the lemon and cherries.

PREP TIP: For an extra-frothy top, instead of a dry shake, Morgenthaler suggests using an immersion blender to first mix all of the ingredients with the egg white, then shake with ice as instructed.

Tools needed: Rocks/old fashioned glass, jigger, bar spoon, shaker, strainer, peeler

Caipirinha

Sweet, Sour

Cachaça is a distilled spirit made exclusively in Brazil from fermented sugarcane juice. It is also the star ingredient in Brazil's most famous cocktail and national drink, the Caipirinha. When cachaça was first imported to the states, and up until 2013, it was often labeled as "Brazilian rum." However, this typically unaged spirit has a fresh fruit quality and a distinctive vegetal character that puts it in a category of its own. Try it as the base spirit in a Manhattan (page 116) instead of whiskey, or in a refreshing highball with ginger beer or tonic.

2 teaspoons sugar

1 lime, cut into wedges

2 ounces cachaça

Lime wheel, for garnish

In a glass, muddle the sugar and lime wedges. Add ice and the cachaça and stir. Garnish with the lime wheel.

DID YOU KNOW? Although the origins of the Caipirinha are unclear, there is one theory that a variation of the cocktail was used as a medicinal remedy for the Spanish Flu epidemic of 1918.

Tools needed: Rocks/old fashioned glass, bar spoon, muddler, paring knife, jigger, bar spoon

Frosé

Sweet, Makes 6 drinks

In the scorching summer of 2016, a pink, frothy, frozen libation swept the country and, seemingly overnight, every restaurant and bar had their own version of blush-colored concoctions. With the rising temps and the perfect portmanteau of frozen plus rosé, the stars aligned and Frosé was born. Justin Sievers, the general manager of Bar Primi in New York City, is responsible for this summertime favorite.

1 bottle full-bodied, dry rosé wine

2 cups frozen strawberries

2 ounces freshly squeezed lemon juice

1 cup dry vermouth

½ cup Simple Syrup (page 135)

1 cup ice

Fresh strawberries, for garnish

Pour the rosé into ice-cube trays and freeze for 6 to 12 hours. Once frozen, combine the rosé cubes in a blender with the frozen strawberries, lemon juice, vermouth, simple syrup, and ice. Blend until smooth and pour into the wine glasses. Garnish with the fresh strawberries.

PREP TIP: If you don't have time to freeze the rosé ahead of time, add a total of 4 cups of ice with the rest of the ingredients when blending.

Tools needed: Wine glasses, ice-cube trays, blender, measuring cups, jigger, paring knife

Grasshopper

Sweet

The Grasshopper's equal-parts combination of artificially green crème de menthe, crème de cacao, and heavy cream feels like another sweet and flashy 1970s drink. It is actually a pre-Prohibition classic, with roots in New Orleans, invented in the early 1900s. This version has an additional ounce of brandy to give this dessert in a glass a bit more backbone.

1 ounce brandy

1 ounce green crème de menthe

1 ounce white crème de cacao

1 ounce heavy (whipping) cream

2 mint sprigs, for garnish

Measure the brandy, crème de menthe, crème de cacao, and heavy cream into a shaker and fill with ice. Shake vigorously. Strain into a chilled glass. Garnish with the mint sprigs.

PREP TIP: For the full dessert treatment, forgo the fresh mint and grate some dark chocolate on top.

Tools needed: Coupe glass, jigger, shaker, strainer

Sake Lychee Martini

Dry

Sake's production process is closer to beer-making than wine, using a yeast-like mold enzyme called koji to ferment the rice. Sake is less acidic than wine, making it a good match with a variety of flavors, including citrus. The Lychee Martini was a 1990s creation when Asian fusion was all the rage, and vodka was the cocktail spirit of choice. This is often made with just vodka and lychee juice reserved from a can of lychee fruit. This version takes advantage of the savory and floral quality of sake to highlight the rose-like aromatics in the lychee.

3 ounces dry sake

1 ounce lychee juice (from a can of lychee fruit)

½ ounce dry vermouth

1 lychee fruit, for garnish

Measure the sake, lychee juice, and vermouth into a shaker with ice. Shake until well chilled. Strain into a chilled glass. Garnish with the lychee fruit.

VARIATION TIP: The base can easily be changed out in this drink. An agave spirit like mezcal or tequila would work well with the sweet and floral lychee juice. Add a pinch of salt to highlight these opposing flavors.

Tools needed: Nick and Nora glass, jigger, shaker, strainer

Chilcano

Sweet, Sour

This cocktail is a simple highball made with pisco (a brandy produced in Peru and Chile), ginger ale, and lime juice. If you're feeling fancy, some cocktail bitters might sneak in. This Peruvian favorite is also a source of national pride. While the Pisco Sour may be the national drink and the most famous cocktail to come out of the country, the locals prefer this simple refresher. This version swaps out the ginger ale for our handmade Ginger Syrup and soda.

2 ounces pisco

¾ ounce freshly squeezed lime juice

¾ ounce Ginger Syrup (page 136)

2 or 3 dashes aromatic bitters

Club soda

Lime wedge, for garnish

Measure the pisco, lime juice, ginger syrup, and bitters into an ice-filled shaker. Shake until chilled. Strain into a glass filled with ice. Top with soda and stir. Garnish with the lime wedge.

PREP TIP: In place of the Ginger Syrup and soda, you can also use 3 to 5 ounces of quality ginger ale.

Tools needed: Highball/Collins glass, jigger, shaker, strainer, bar spoon, paring knife

The Adonis

Dry

This classic aperitif was created at the Waldorf-Astoria Hotel in New York City in the late 1800s and named in honor of the longest running Broadway musical at the time. While the Adonis may be the most well-known sherry-based cocktail, it is still an under-the-radar sipper. Low in alcohol, simple to make but quite nuanced, this drink is a perfect pre-dinner "stomach opener."

2 ounces fino sherry

1½ ounces sweet vermouth

2 dashes orange bitters

Orange peel, for garnish

Tools needed:
Nick and Nora glass, jigger, mixing glass, bar spoon, strainer, peeler

Measure the sherry, sweet vermouth, and bitters into a mixing glass filled with ice. Stir until well chilled. Strain into a chilled glass. Express orange oils from the peel over the drink and add the peel as a garnish.

PREP TIP: Some recipes call for the sherry and sweet vermouth to be equal parts. Adjust the ratios, according to your taste. This cocktail varies greatly, depending on the kind of sweet vermouth you use. Carpano Antica will be drier and more savory, while Dolin or Tempus Fugit will yield a more fruit-forward cocktail.

Yuzu Sour

Strong

Like sake, shōchū is native to Japan, has a long and storied history, and uses koji, the same fermentation starter used in making miso or soy sauce. But unlike sake, shōchū is a distilled spirit, most similar to vodka, as it can be made from everything from sweet potatoes to barley to black sugarcane. It is the national spirit of Japan and outsells sake by 50 percent there, but it is still fairly unknown in the States. Shōchū has a dry, earthy quality that makes it highly adaptable as a base spirit. In this sour, the shōchū lends structure but ultimately blends into the background as the citrus, honey, and ginger become the focal point. The splash of seltzer adds a light and refreshing topper.

2 ounces shōchū

¾ ounce Honey Ginger Syrup (page 136)

½ ounce yuzu juice (see tip)

¼ ounce freshly squeezed lemon juice

Splash seltzer

Lemon wedge, for garnish

Measure the shōchū, honey ginger syrup, yuzu juice, and lemon juice into a shaker with ice. Shake until well chilled. Strain into an ice-filled wine glass. Top with seltzer, and garnish with the lemon wedge.

PREP TIP: Yuzu is a hybrid variety of citrus also referred to as *yuja*, thought to have originated in China over 1,000 years ago. Extremely aromatic and more sour than most citrus, the flavor is a cross between a lemon and a grapefruit, either of which can be used if yuzu is not available.

> **Tools needed:** Wine glass, jigger, shaker, strainer, paring knife

CHAPTER 10
Syrups, Mixers & Modifiers

What makes a cocktail... a *cocktail?* Most definitions are pretty broad, often as simple as an alcoholic base spirit mixed with other ingredients. Those other ingredients are there to complement that base. Ingredients that support the main spirit in a cocktail usually contain alcohol. These ingredients, such as sweet liqueurs or fortified wines and vermouths, are considered modifiers. Modifiers not only add depth of flavor to a drink, they also alter the mouthfeel and the overall alcohol content. Fresh juice and quality syrups, mixers, and modifiers are as important as the star ingredient. All of the recipes offered here are featured heavily as cocktail ingredients throughout this book.

Simple Syrup 135

Ginger Syrup & Honey Ginger Variation 136

Earl Grey Syrup 137

Coffee Syrup 138

Orgeat Syrup 139

Limoncello 140

Bloody Mary Mix 141

Coffee Liqueur 142

Simple Syrup

Makes about 1½ cups

Simple syrup may be the most used ingredient when crafting cocktails, especially when citrus is involved. Luckily, it's easy to make! Superfine sugar tends to dissolve more quickly into syrups than granulated sugar does. If using demerara sugar, reduce the water by half.

1 cup sugar

1 cup water

In a small saucepan over low to medium heat, combine the sugar and water and stir until the sugar is fully dissolved. Cool completely. Transfer to a sealable jar or bottle and refrigerate for up to a month.

> **Tools needed:** Saucepan, measuring cup, bar spoon, sealable jar or bottle

Ginger Syrup & Honey Ginger Variation

Makes about 1 cup

Infusing a simple syrup with different fruits, roots, or herbs is the easiest way to change up a cocktail's flavor profile. This ginger syrup can be made with a toffee-like demerara sugar or honey for an especially rich syrup.

- 1 cup demerara sugar or honey
- ½ cup water
- ½ cup diced unpeeled ginger root

In a small saucepan over medium heat, combine the sugar, water, and ginger and simmer for 5 minutes. Remove from the heat and cool completely. Place in the refrigerator to steep overnight. Strain the ginger out with a fine-mesh strainer. Transfer the syrup to a sealable jar or bottle and refrigerate for up to a month.

Tools needed: Saucepan, measuring cups, fine-mesh strainer, sealable jar or bottle

Earl Grey Syrup

Makes 1 cup

One of the easiest ways to infuse a simple syrup with flavors is to use tea bags or loose-leaf tea. This heady bergamot syrup is surprisingly versatile and works especially well with the botanicals in gin.

1 tablespoon loose-leaf Earl Grey tea or 1 tea bag

1 cup water

1 cup sugar

In a small saucepan over medium heat, combine the tea and water and bring to a boil. Remove from the heat, add the sugar, and steep for 4 or 5 minutes. Strain the tea leaves out with a fine-mesh strainer and set the syrup aside to cool completely. Transfer to a sealable jar or bottle and refrigerate for up to a month.

Tools needed: Saucepan, tablespoon, measuring cup, fine-mesh strainer, sealable jar or bottle

Coffee Syrup

Makes about 1½ cups

The key to a great-tasting coffee syrup is using quality, freshly ground coffee beans. This rich syrup works especially well with whiskey and agave spirits.

½ cup dark roast whole coffee beans

1 cup water

1 cup sugar

In a coffee grinder or food processor, finely grind the coffee beans. In a small saucepan over medium heat, bring the water to a boil. Remove from the heat, add the sugar and coffee grounds, and steep for 4 or 5 minutes. Strain the coffee grounds out through a coffee filter and set the syrup aside to cool completely. Transfer to a sealable jar or bottle and refrigerate for up to a month.

Tools needed: Coffee grinder, measuring cups, saucepan, coffee filter, sealable jar or bottle

Orgeat Syrup

Makes about 2 cups

Orgeat syrup, commonly used in classic cocktails and tiki drinks, is an almond-flavored syrup with a touch of floral aromatics. The orange flower water, made from orange blossoms, is a key flavoring component. It can be found online and in most upscale food markets.

- 2 cups blanched almonds
- 1½ cups sugar
- 1¼ cups water
- 1 teaspoon orange flower water
- 1 ounce vodka

Tools needed: Food processor, measuring cups, saucepan, bar spoon, cheesecloth, bowl, jigger, sealable jar or bottle

In a food processor, grind the almonds to a coarse powder. In a medium saucepan over medium heat, combine the sugar and water and bring to a boil. Add the ground almonds, stirring constantly for 3 minutes. Reduce the heat to low, continue stirring, and simmer for 3 minutes more. Remove the saucepan from the heat, cover it with a lid, and set it aside to infuse for 4 to 6 hours at room temperature. Strain the almond mixture by squeezing it through three layers of cheesecloth into a bowl. Discard the almond pulp. Add the orange flower water and vodka to the almond syrup and stir. Transfer to a sealable jar or bottle and refrigerate for up to 2 weeks.

Limoncello

Makes about 5 cups

Limoncello is a traditional southern Italian liqueur made from lemon peels. It is excellent on its own, served very cold, after a meal, or as a sweet cocktail modifier.

10 lemons (ideally organic)

1 (750-milliliter) bottle high-proof, grain alcohol (such as Everclear)

2 cups Simple Syrup (page 135)

Peel the lemon skins very thin, avoiding the pith (the white part closest to the fruit) to prevent bitterness. Place the peels in a large canister. Add the alcohol to the canister. Cover and set aside in a dark, cool spot to infuse for 2 weeks. After 2 weeks, strain the lemon peels from the alcohol. Add the simple syrup to the alcohol and store for at least 1 month in a dark, cool spot for the flavors to mellow. Transfer into bottles with a funnel and store in the refrigerator or freezer for up to a month.

Tools needed: Peeler, large canister, measuring cup, strainer, bottles, funnel

Bloody Mary Mix

Makes 8 servings

This large batch of Bloody Mary Mix is created to be a savory balance of just the right amount of citrus, seasoning, and heat for an easy-to-prepare Bloody Mary (page 95).

- 4 cups tomato juice
- ¼ cup freshly squeezed lemon juice
- 2 tablespoons freshly grated horseradish
- 2 tablespoons Worcestershire sauce
- 2 tablespoons celery salt
- 1 tablespoon hot sauce
- 1 tablespoon ground black pepper
- 1 teaspoon smoked paprika
- Salt, for seasoning

Measure the tomato juice, lemon juice, horseradish, Worcestershire sauce, celery salt, hot sauce, pepper, and paprika into a pitcher or sealable canister and stir. Cover and refrigerate for up to 2 days.

Tools needed: Measuring cups, citrus squeezer, tablespoon, bar spoon, pitcher

Coffee Liqueur

Makes about 5 cups

Coffee-infused rum or brandy mixed with Simple Syrup (page 135) makes for an easy and delicious liqueur. Make sure to use a real vanilla bean for dimension and authentic vanilla flavor.

1 cup dark roast whole coffee beans

1 vanilla bean, sliced open

1 bottle rum or brandy

1½ cups Simple Syrup (page 135)

In a coffee grinder or food processor, finely grind the coffee beans. Place the coffee grounds, vanilla bean, and rum in a 1-liter sealable jar. Let this infusion sit for at least 2 days, shaking occasionally. Strain through a coffee filter until the coffee grounds and vanilla bean are removed. Combine the infused rum with the simple syrup. Transfer back to the jar and refrigerate for up to a month.

Tools needed: Coffee grinder, measuring cups, 1-liter jar, coffee filter

Measurement Conversions

Volume Equivalents (Liquid)

US STANDARD	US STANDARD (OUNCES)	METRIC (APPROXIMATE)
2 tablespoons	1 fl. oz.	30 mL
¼ cup	2 fl. oz.	60 mL
½ cup	4 fl. oz.	120 mL
1 cup	8 fl. oz.	240 mL
1½ cups	12 fl. oz.	355 mL
2 cups or 1 pint	16 fl. oz.	475 mL
4 cups or 1 quart	32 fl. oz.	1 L
1 gallon	128 fl. oz.	4 L

Resources

For those of you who want to continue on this cocktail-making journey and expand upon the information provided in this book, there are many excellent resources. Here are the books and websites (including my own!) I look to when researching, sourcing information, and mixing up cocktails myself.

Books

Amaro: The Spirited World of Bittersweet, Herbal Liqueurs by Brad Thomas Parsons

The Artistry of Mixing Drinks by Frank Meier

The Bartender's Guide: How to Mix Drinks or The Bon Vivant's Companion by Jerry Thomas

Cocktail Italiano by Annette Joseph

The Craft Cocktail Party: Delicious Drinks for Every Occasion by Julie Reiner

Death & Co: Modern Classic Cocktails by David Kaplan, Nick Fauchald, and Alex Day

Imbibe! by David Wondrich

The Joy of Mixology by Gary Regan

The New Craft of the Cocktail by Dale DeGroff

The PDT Cocktail Book by Jim Meehan

Regarding Cocktails by Sasha Petraske and Georgette Moger-Petraske

The Savoy Cocktail Book by Harry Craddock

Shake. Stir. Sip. by Kara Newman

Speakeasy by Jason Kosmas and Dushan Zaric

Spirits of Latin America: A Celebration of Culture & Cocktails by Ivy Mix

Tiki: Modern Tropical Cocktails by Shannon Mustipher

Vintage Spirits and Forgotten Cocktails by Ted Haigh

Websites

Alcademics.com

BitByAFox.com

ImbibeMagazine.com

JeffreyMorgenthaler.com

Liquor.com

PunchDrink.com

Index

A

Abou-Ganim, Tony, 76
Absinthe
  Coffee Sazerac, 34–35
  Vanderbilt Stinger, 36–37
The Adonis, 129
Alcohol by volume
  (ABV), 3
Amaretto Sour, 122
Amelia, 104
Amore Mio, 118
Ankrah, Douglas, 93
Aperitifs, 3
Aperol
  Italiano Spritz, 42
  Negroni Sbagliato
    (Mistaken
    Negroni), 47
  Sarong Queen, 71
Artistry of Mixing Drinks,
  The (Meier), 46

B

Bar spoons, 16
Basil Gimlet, 92
Bergeron, Walter, 117
Berry, Jeff, 74
Beyoncé, 112
Bitter aperitivo liqueurs, 8
  Italiano Spritz, 42
  Negroni Sbagliato
    (Mistaken Negroni), 47
  Sarong Queen, 71
Bitters, 3, 13
Blood Orange Mimosa, 46
Bloody Mary, 95
Bloody Mary Mix, 141
Boccato, Richard, 59
Botanical liqueurs, 8
Bottoms Up! (Saucier), 62
Bourbon, 6
  Amaretto Sour, 122
  Amore Mio, 118
  Bourbon Renewal, 111

Paper Plane, 113
The Retox, 112
Seelbach, 49
Bradsell, Dick, 63, 99
Bramble, 63
Brandy, 6, 28
  Brandy Alexander, 39
  Brandy Highball, 33
  Chilcano, 128
  Coffee Liqueur, 142
  Coffee Sazerac, 34–35
  Corpse Reviver No. 1, 38
  Grasshopper, 126
  Jack Rosé Spritz, 31
  Sidecar, 32
  Vanderbilt
    Stinger, 36–37
  Vieux Carré, 117
Brighton Beachcomber, 81
Building, 4, 19

C

Cable Car, 76
Cabrera, Julio, 75
Caipirinha, 123
Campari
  Italiano Spritz, 42
  Jungle Bird, 74
  Negroni Sbagliato
    (Mistaken Negroni), 47
  Negroni Snow Cone, 57
  Sarong Queen, 71
Cardinale, Claudia, 110
Cecchini, Toby, 96
Champagne, 9, 40–41.
    See also Sparkling wines
Chartreuse liqueur
  The Last Word, 62
  Naked & Famous, 87
Chilcano, 128
Cipriani, Giuseppe, 45
Citrus squeezers, 17
Cocktails
  craft, 2–3
  flourishes, 20–21
  formula, 23
  glassware, 15–16
  inventing, 22–24
  naming, 24–25
  step-by-step, 21–22
  techniques, 19–20
  tools, 16–18
Cocktail shakers, 17
Coffee Liqueur, 142
  Amore Mio, 118
  Coffee Old Fashioned, 115
  Espresso Martini, 99
  The Fabergé (A White
    Russian Egg
    Cream), 105
  The Veracruz, 86
Coffee Sazerac, 34–35
Coffee Syrup, 138
Cognac
  Corpse Reviver No. 1, 38
Cointreau
  Cosmopolitan, 96–97
  Flatiron Martini, 103
  Jalapeño Cucumber
    Margarita, 83–84
  Seelbach, 49
  Water Lily, 59
Collins glasses, 15
Conigliaro, Tony, 50
Corpse Reviver No. 1, 38
Cosmonaut, 61
Cosmopolitan, 96–97
Coupe glasses, 15
Craddock, Harry, 38, 61
Craft cocktails, defined, 2–3
Crème de cacao
  Brandy Alexander, 39
  Grasshopper, 126
Crème de menthe
  Grasshopper, 126
  Vanderbilt Stinger, 36–37

D

Dash, 4
DeGroff, Dale, 55
Dry shaking, 19

E

Earl Grey MarTEAni, 60
Earl Grey Syrup, 137
Elderflower liqueur
  Amelia, 104
  Twinkle, 50
El Presidente, 75
Espresso Martini, 99
Expressing, 4

F

The Fabergé (A White
  Russian Egg
  Cream), 105

Flatiron Martini, 103
Floating, 4
Flourishes, 20–21
Fortified wines, 9
French 75, 43
Frosé, 125
Fruit liqueurs, 8
Fruits, 11–12, 13

G

Galliano
   Harvey Wallbanger Slushy, 98
Garnishes, 4, 12–15, 20–21
Gin, 7, 52
   Bramble, 63
   Cosmonaut, 61
   Earl Grey MarTEAni, 60
   French 75, 43
   Ginger Bee's Knees, 56
   Gin-Gin Mule, 55
   The Last Word, 62
   Limoncello Gin & Tonic, 54
   Martini, 64–65
   Negroni Snow Cone, 57
   Water Lily, 59
Ginger Bee's Knees, 56
Ginger Syrup, 136
Glassware, 15–16
González, Giuseppe, 109
Grand Marnier
   Limoncello Drop, 100–101
Grasshopper, 126

H

Harry's ABC of Mixing Cocktails (MacElhone), 92
Harvey Wallbanger Slushy, 98
Hemingway Daiquiri, 70
Herbal liqueurs, 8
Highball glasses, 15
Hobday, Norman Jay, 100
Honey Ginger Syrup, 136

I

Ice, 14
Improved Midori Sour, 102
Intoxica! (Berry), 74
Italiano Spritz, 42

J

Jack Rosé Spritz, 31
Jalapeño Cucumber Margarita, 83–84
Jiggers, 17, 18
Juices, 11–12
Jungle Bird, 74

K

Kosmas, Jason, 104

L

Lamour, Dorothy, 71
The Last Word, 62
Lillet Blanc
   Flatiron Martini, 103
Limoncello, 140
   Limoncello Drop, 100–101
   Limoncello Gin & Tonic, 54
Liqueurs, 4, 8
Liquors, 6–7. *See also* specific

M

MacElhone, Harry, 92
Mango con Chili Bellini, 45
Manhattan, 116
Marrero, Ramón, 73
Martini, 64–65
   Earl Grey MarTEAni, 60
   Espresso Martini, 99
   Flatiron Martini, 103

Martini (*continued*)
  Porn Star Martini, 93
  Sake Lychee
    Martini, 127
Meier, Frank, 46
Mezcal, 7, 78
  Mezcal Paloma, 85
  Naked & Famous, 87
  Oaxaca Old Fashioned, 88
  Tía Mía, 89
Midori Sour, Improved, 102
Mix, Ivy, 89
Mixers, 4, 9–12
Mixing glasses, 17
Mixologists, 2
Modifiers, 4
Moger-Petraske,
  Georgette, 59
Mojito, 69
Monsoon Slushy, 68
Morgenthaler, Jeffrey,
  111, 122
Muddlers, 17, 18
Muddling, 5

N

Naked & Famous, 87
Neat, 5

Negroni Sbagliato (Mistaken
  Negroni), 47
Negroni Snow Cone, 57
Nick and Nora glasses, 16

O

Oaxaca Old Fashioned, 88
Old Cuban, 48
Old fashioned glasses, 16
On the rocks, 5
Orange liqueur.
    See also Cointreau
  Sidecar, 32
  Water Lily, 59
Orgeat Syrup, 139

P

Paper Plane, 113
Paring knives, 17
Peelers, 17
Penicillin, 108
Petiot, Fernand, 95
Petraske, Sasha, 59, 61, 113
Peychaud, Antoine
  Amédée, 34
Piña Colada, 73
Porn Star Martini, 93
Proof, 3

Prosecco
  Italiano Spritz, 42
  Negroni Sbagliato
    (Mistaken Negroni), 47

R

Ranch Water, 80
Recipes, about, 26
Reiner, Julie, 103
The Retox, 112
Rinsing the glass, 20
Rocks, 5
Rocks glasses, 16
Rolling, 19
Rosé wine
  Frosé, 125
  Jack Rosé Spritz, 31
Ross, Sam, 108, 113
Rum, 7, 66
  Cable Car, 76
  Coffee Liqueur, 142
  El Presidente, 75
  Hemingway Daiquiri, 70
  Jungle Bird, 74
  Mojito, 69
  Monsoon Slushy, 68
  Old Cuban, 48
  Piña Colada, 73

Sarong Queen, 71
Tía Mía, 89
Rye, 6. *See also* Whiskey/whisky

S

Sake Lychee Martini, 127
Sarong Queen, 71
Saucier, Ted, 62
Saunders, Audrey, 48, 55, 60
Savoy Cocktail Book, The (Craddock), 38
Scotch, 6
  Penicillin, 108
Seelbach, 49
Seger, Adam, 49
Shakers, 17, 18
Shaking, 5, 19, 20
Sherry
  The Adonis, 129
Shōchū
  Yuzu Sour, 130–131
Sidecar, 32
Sievers, Justin, 125
Simó, Joaquín, 87
Simple Syrup, 135
Sodas, 10–11
Sparkling wines, 9, 40–41

Blood Orange Mimosa, 46
French 75, 43
Italiano Spritz, 42
Mango con Chili Bellini, 45
Negroni Sbagliato (Mistaken Negroni), 47
Old Cuban, 48
Porn Star Martini, 93
Seelbach, 49
Twinkle, 50
Stenson, Murray, 62
Stirring, 5, 20
Straight-up, 5
Strainers, 17, 18
Straining, 5, 19
Sweeteners, 9–10
Syrups, 9–10
  Coffee Syrup, 138
  Earl Grey Syrup, 137
  Ginger Syrup, 136
  Honey Ginger Syrup, 136
  Orgeat Syrup, 139
  Simple Syrup, 135

T

Techniques, 19–20
Tequila, 7, 78
  Brighton Beachcomber, 81

Jalapeño Cucumber Margarita, 83–84
Oaxaca Old Fashioned, 88
Ranch Water, 80
The Veracruz, 86
Thomas, Jerry, 32
Tía Mía, 89
Tools, 16–18
Top with, 5
Trinidad Sour, 109
Twinkle, 50

U

Up, 5

V

Vanderbilt, Reginald, 36
Vanderbilt Stinger, 36–37
The Veracruz, 86
Vermouth
  The Adonis, 129
  Corpse Reviver No. 1, 38
  El Presidente, 75
  Frosé, 125
  Manhattan, 116
  Martini, 64–65
  Negroni Sbagliato (Mistaken Negroni), 47

Vermouth (*continued*)
  Negroni Snow Cone, 57
  Sake Lychee Martini, 127
  Vieux Carré, 117
Vieux Carré, 117
Vodka, 7, 90–91
  Amelia, 104
  Basil Gimlet, 92
  Bloody Mary, 95
  Cosmopolitan, 96–97
  Espresso Martini, 99
  The Fabergé (A White
    Russian Egg Cream), 105
  Flatiron Martini, 103
  Harvey Wallbanger
    Slushy, 98
  Improved Midori Sour, 102
  Limoncello Drop, 100–101
  Porn Star Martini, 93
  Twinkle, 50

W

Ward, Phil, 88
Washing the glass, 20
Water Lily, 59
Whiskey/whisky, 6, 106–107
  Coffee Old Fashioned, 115
  Manhattan, 116
  Trinidad Sour, 109
  Vieux Carré, 117
  Whiskey Cardinale, 110
Wine glasses, 16

Y

Yuzu Sour, 130–131

Z

Zaric, Dushan, 104

Acknowledgments

I'd like to thank my editor, Anna Pulley, for so deftly handling this first-time author's cocktail nerdisms and patiently holding my hand throughout this process. Some very special *Foxy Friends* that I'd like to acknowledge, who have been incredibly supportive of me and *Bit by a Fox* through the years (not to mention, very astute cocktail taste testers): Joy Barrett, Aime Graham, Shannon Carpenter, Rose Callahan, Cristina Kovacs, Pi James, Mary Unruh, Natalie Sandoval, Karen Parker, Guido Venitucci, Angela Lovell, Jonni Swensen, Eileen O'Dea, Catharine Dill, DeAnna Lenhart, Trinity Croghan, Kerry and Scot Armstrong, Raina and Jesse Falcon, Nickie Tiedeman and Morgan Visconti, Michael and Calvin Cruz, Lee Houck and Kip Rathke, Ashley Smith and Dave Steele, Rob and Sandy Corddry; *Elegant Ladies*, Cristina Santos, Tammy Henault, Maria Betances, Mindy Troutman, Rasanah Goss; *Boozy Babe*, Emily Arden Wells; and my sister in gin, Georgette Moger-Petraske. Finally, thanks to my mom, Barbara Zelano, who continues to support my boozy endeavors and whose palate has come a long way from those '80s kamikazes.

About the Author

 **Prairie Rose** is an LA-based drinks writer, trained sommelier, wine and spirits educator, and podcast host. She is the founder and editor of *Bit by a Fox*, winner of *Saveur* magazine's Readers' Choice Award for Best Drinks Blog, and the producer and host of the *Bit by a Fox Podcast*, now in its fourth season. In October 2020, she joined drinks website *Liquor.com* as Commerce Editor.

CPSIA information can be obtained
at www.ICGtesting.com
Printed in the USA
BVHW062218181221
624451BV00019B/1949